CALUMET CITY PUBLIC LIBRARY

3 1613 00450 5650

P9-CCJ-486

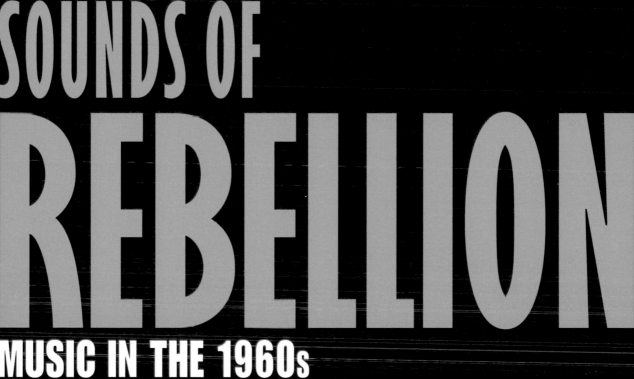

SOUNDS OF
REBELLION
MUSIC IN THE 1960s

POPULAR MUSIC
THROUGH THE DECADES

SOUNDS OF
REBELLION

MUSIC IN THE 1960s

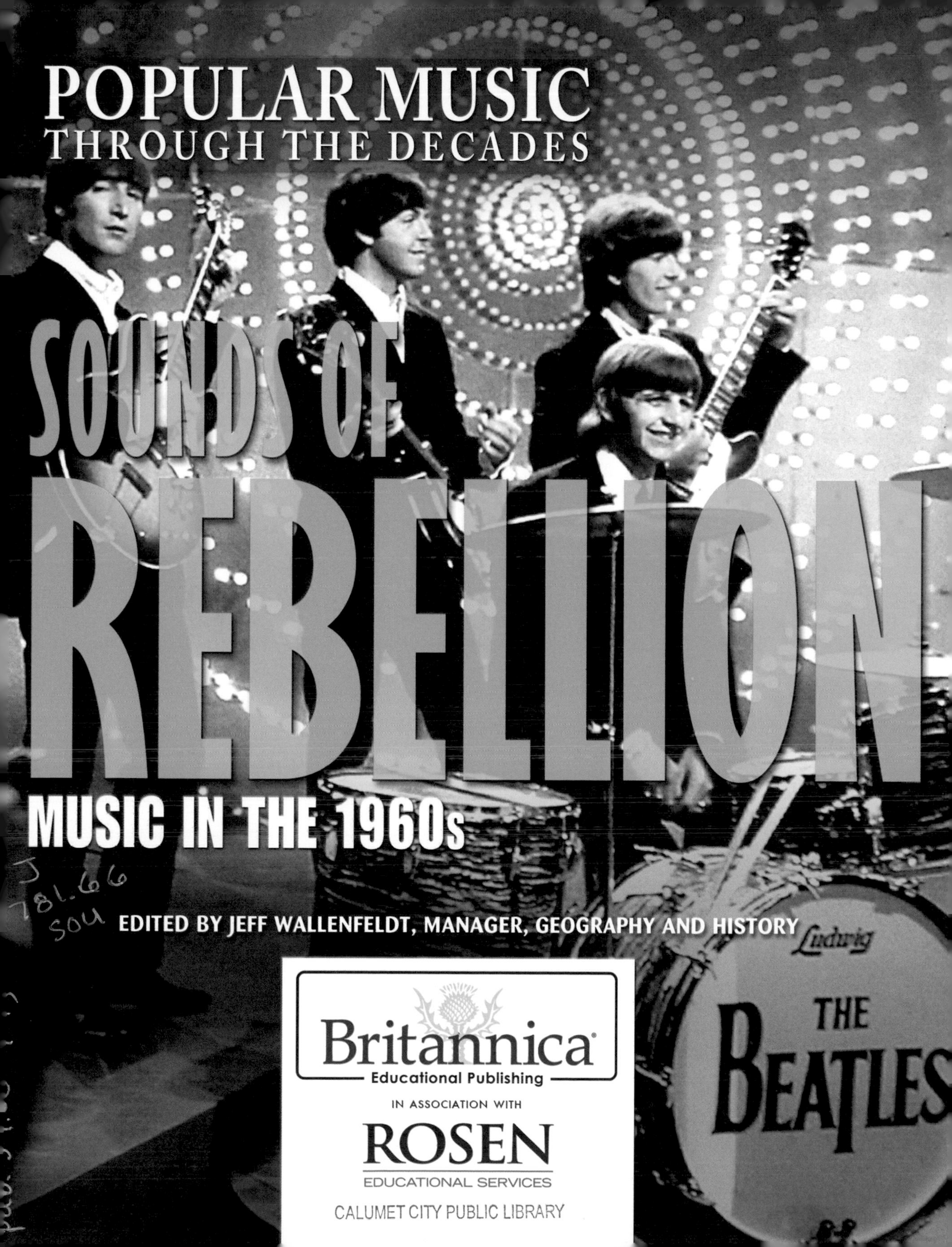

J
781.66
SOU

EDITED BY JEFF WALLENFELDT, MANAGER, GEOGRAPHY AND HISTORY

Britannica®
Educational Publishing

IN ASSOCIATION WITH

ROSEN
EDUCATIONAL SERVICES

CALUMET CITY PUBLIC LIBRARY

Ludwig

THE
BEATLES

Published in 2013 by Britannica Educational Publishing
(a trademark of Encyclopædia Britannica, Inc.) in association with Rosen Educational Services, LLC

29 East 21st Street, New York, NY 10010.

Copyright © 2013 Encyclopædia Britannica, Inc. Britannica, Encyclopædia Britannica, and the Thistle logo are registered trademarks of Encyclopædia Britannica, Inc. All rights reserved.

Rosen Educational Services materials copyright © 2013 Rosen Educational Services, LLC. All rights reserved.

Distributed exclusively by Rosen Educational Services.
For a listing of additional Britannica Educational Publishing titles, call toll free (800) 237-9932.

First Edition

Britannica Educational Publishing
J.E. Luebering: Senior Manager
Adam Augustyn: Assistant Manager
Marilyn L. Barton: Senior Coordinator, Production Control
Steven Bosco: Director, Editorial Technologies
Lisa S. Braucher: Senior Producer and Data Editor
Yvette Charboneau: Senior Copy Editor
Kathy Nakamura: Manager, Media Acquisition
Jeff Wallenfeldt, Manager, Geography and History

Rosen Educational Services
Shalini Saxena: Editor
Nelson Sá: Art Director
Cindy Reiman: Photography Manager
Karen Huang: Photo Researcher
Brian Garvey: Designer, Cover Design
Introduction by Jeff Wallenfeldt

Library of Congress Cataloging-in-Publication Data

Sounds of rebellion: music in the 1960s/edited by Jeff Wallenfeldt.—1st ed.
    p. cm.—(Popular music through the decades)
"In association with Britannica Educational Publishing, Rosen Educational Services."
Includes bibliographical references and index.
ISBN 978-1-61530-907-8 (library binding)
1. Popular music—1961-1970—History and criticism. I. Wallenfeldt, Jeffrey H.
ML3470.S636 2013
781.6409'046—dc23

2012020472

Manufactured in the United States of America

On the cover, p. iii: The Beatles performing on the British television show, *Top of the Pops*, in 1966. From left to right: John Lennon, Paul McCartney, Ringo Starr, and George Harrison. *Ron Howard/Redferns/Getty Images*

Pages 1, 13, 24, 32, 44, 60, 74, 89, 112, 124, 145, 168 Ethan Miller/Getty Images (Fender Stratocaster guitar), iStockphoto.com/catrinka81 (treble clef graphic); interior background image iStockphoto.com/hepatus; back cover © iStockphoto.com/Vladimir Jajin

CONTENTS

47

50

71

122

128

141

163

170

173

Introduction

At more than eight minutes long, singer-songwriter Don McLean's "American Pie" was an unlikely hit on AM radio when it topped the Billboard Hot 100 chart in 1972, yet for many teenagers at the time committing all six of the song's verses to memory was a rite of passage. Those lyrics offered a mythic explanation of some 10 tumultuous years in the history of the United States, the counterculture, and popular music, stretching roughly from rock-and-roll star Buddy Holly's death in a plane crash in 1959 to the debacle at the Altamont music festival helplessly presided over by the Rolling Stones in 1969. It was a period during which the rebelliousness that had been so central to early rock and roll returned after having disappeared at the end of the 1950s, when it was largely replaced by the sanitized pretty-boy pleasantness of teen icons such as Frankie Avalon and Fabian. The rebellion of 1950s rockers had seldom been articulated by them; it was more a matter of gesture, but gestures that meant everything. The embracement of black music and musicians and the adaptation of black musical styles by a growing number of white Americans had revolutionary implications. Rock-and-roll shows that attracted mixed black–and-white audiences were implicit sallies on segregation. But in the 1960s popular music's discontent with the status quo found its voice and became ideological, mirroring a generation's assault on the politics, culture, and economics of post-World War II society.

The era's folk music revival was catalyzed by a group of clean-cut collegiate-looking guys in matching shirts (the Kingston Trio) who wowed Middle America with polished versions of traditional songs. In short order, however, the legion of newly minted folkies who strummed their acoustic guitars in Washington Square in New York City began to embrace the progressive political mission that was the legacy of the old left and the old folkies who had kept the fires of dissent burning in Greenwich Village during the McCarthy era and the early Cold War years. In the 1950s screen idol James Dean had embodied the emphatic but inchoate angst of generation of young people who felt something was wrong with the way they were expected to live, but he was a "Rebel Without a Cause." In the 1960s, young people and musicians took up and spoke forcefully about a number of causes, beginning with the civil rights movement.

Bob Dylan (generally taken to be the jester in "American Pie," who sings in a coat borrowed from James Dean and "voice that came from you and me") became the darling of the folk revival by updating traditional song forms with poetically complex, politically infused lyrics that confronted the discrimination and duplicity in American society head on. He and others who shared his political concerns—most notably "singing journalist" Phil Ochs—became "protest" singers. Dylan and Joan Baez performed on the steps of the Lincoln Memorial before the Rev. Martin Luther King, Jr., delivered his famous "I Have a Dream" speech during the March on Washington in 1963; later, Ochs—whose opposition to the Vietnam War was legendary—helped form the Youth International Party and was at the centre of Yippie demonstrations at the cataclysmic national convention of the Democratic Party in Chicago in 1968.

As the decade progressed, Dylan and American youth in general heard another clarion call, sounded from across the Atlantic by British "beat" groups who echoed the power of early American rock and roll. Liverpool,

a once-majestic imperial port city in economic decline, was the home to hundreds of these groups. In an atmosphere of postwar austerity that had limited the leisure options for young Britons in the 1950s, skiffle music provided an exciting alternative. The material requirements were minimal: one or more acoustic guitars and a rudimentary bass, often fashioned from a broomstick attached to a tea chest. The music sources were American folk and blues. Lonnie Donegan, a member of a band that played traditional New Orleans-style jazz (Britain's other great musical preoccupation at the time) became skiffle's avatar when his rendition of American folk-blues singer Leadbelly's "Rock Island Line" was a hit in 1954. The skiffle groups that sprang up across the United Kingdom began looking beyond folk and blues to rhythm and blues and early rock and roll for their sources. This was especially true in Liverpool, to which, according to the most romantic version of the movement's origins, the "Cunard Yanks"—the stewards and those who worked on passenger ships—returned from the United States with the latest R&B and rock-and-roll hit records, as well as electric guitars. Teenage Liverpudlian skiffle players, such as future Beatles John Lennon and Paul McCartney, fell in the thrall of Elvis Presley, Chuck Berry, Little

Richard, Carl Perkins, and especially Buddy Holly, whose stylish but relatively straightforward guitar playing was imitable. The "beat boom," the British reinvention of rock and roll, and the "invasion" of the United States by British groups were but a few hundred amplifiers away.

At the centre of this British invasion were the Beatles, who honed their musical chops with marathon sets in clubs on the Reeperbahn strip in Hamburg, Germany, and held court in Liverpool's Cavern Club. Not only were they impassioned vocalists and skilled players, but they were boundlessly, joyfully energetic, witty, and clever. They were good looking, too, though they did not look like anyone else, having traded in their leather jackets and pompadours for modish matching suits and long-banged "French-style" haircuts that earned them the nickname "mop tops," which only added to their appeal. None of this was lost on the young females who screamed throughout their concerts as the "Fab Four's" hits multiplied and the frenzied fandom that became known as Beatlemania swept Britain, the United States, and the world. At the same time, in becoming national icons in Britain, the Beatles helped fell class barriers and sweep away notions of provincial backwardness. In the process, the Beatles and the other British beat groups who "invaded" the United

States beginning in early 1964 reintroduced Americans to rock and roll, becoming the second act in a transatlantic cross-pop-cultural exchange that is still taking place.

Like the Beatles, London's Rolling Stones were connoisseurs of American music, though in the case of the Stones, at least initially, blues and rhythm and blues were their passion. Indeed, London was the fulcrum of a British blues movement that also included John Mayall's Bluesbreakers and the Yardbirds. The Rolling Stones took their name from a song by Chicago electric bluesman Muddy Waters and worshipped at the temple of Howlin' Wolf, Robert Johnson, Elmore James, and Little Walter, among others. The Stones cultivated a bad-boy image and, with the exception of the goldilocked Brian Jones, were uglyish where the Beatles where irrepressibly cute. Yet the Stones conveyed a seductive hypersexuality, especially lead singer Mick Jagger, who preened and strutted on stage like the eponymous little red rooster of the song that was one of their early signature recordings. Like Lennon and other breakthrough artists from the period (most notably Pete Townshend of the Who and Eric Clapton), members of the Stones (guitarist Keith Richards and drummer Charlie Watts) also attended art schools, which proved to be perfect hothouses for the creation of

British rock and roll. It took Jagger and Richards longer to begin writing their own songs than it had Lennon and McCartney, who, early on, began developing their extraordinary talents as songwriters. Ultimately it was the fact that they wrote their own songs that set the Beatles apart from almost all pop musicians who came before them in the era when professional songwriters wrote songs and singers performed them.

The mutual influence of the Beatles and Dylan upon each other was pivotal to the development of rock and roll as an art form. With his increasingly sophisticated and poetic lyrics, Dylan showed the Beatles that pop songs could be so much more than Moon-June-rhyming paeans to new romance or homilies to heartbreak. They could, in fact, be about anything, including politics, the profound, and the profane. Thus inspired the Beatles retreated from touring (tired of trying to be heard over concert audiences' screaming) and with their essential collaborator, producer George Martin, took to the studio to create a series of sonically and compositionally adventurous albums that pushed the boundaries of popular music beyond even the most distant horizons. In the meantime, the Beatles dazzled Dylan and reminded him of his teenage infatuation with rock and roll (his high school yearbook had memorialized

his desire "to join Little Richard"). Dylan then shocked the folk world by going electric and pursuing the "wild mercury sound" that would be his version of rock and roll. And he was not alone; seemingly overnight in the mid-1960s America was awash in Beatlized Dylans, folkies who plugged in electric guitars and began to rock—not least the Byrds, Buffalo Springfield, Simon and Garfunkel, the Lovin' Spoonful, and the Mamas & the Papas. Just as Dylan began to turn inward and away from politics, many of these folk rockers took on the problems of a society they believed was, as Barry McGuire sang, "on the eve of destruction."

Growing opposition to the Vietnam War united the two principal branches of the burgeoning youth-oriented counterculture: the hippies, whose rejection of middle-class mores and materialism was an outgrowth of the bohemianism of the 1950s Beat Movement and the embracement of eastern philosophy and psychedelic consciousness (more on this in a moment); and the New Left, whose radical pursuit of economic and direct democracy was for a time steered by the Students for a Democratic Society. The New Left also continued to be involved in the civil rights movement, which evolved throughout the 1960s from a nonviolent action seeking civil rights goals and legislation into a broader

Folk musicians attract listeners of all ages in New York City's Washington Square Park, the centre of the folk revival, in 1961. © AP Images

freedom struggle grounded in "black power," some of whose members, frustrated by the slow pace of progress, were willing to use "any means necessary" to achieve a more equitable society.

Soul music, the impassioned, gospel-rooted African American music that had arisen after rock and roll's appropriation of rhythm and blues, provided the soundtrack and inspiration for this struggle. Backed by his impossibly funky band the Famous Flames, James Brown, the "Godfather of Soul," took syncopation to new levels in the service of black pride; Aretha Franklin, the "Queen of Soul," demanded "respect" for women and their rights with every note she sang; and Curtis Mayfield made it abundantly clear that it was well past time for African Americans to "move on up." A surfeit of soul music for the ages was created in Memphis, first at Stax Records' movie theatre-turned-recording studio and then at Hi Records. At Stax, a gifted interracial house band (essentially Booker T. and the MGs) and a group of immensely talented performer-writer-producers, including Isaac Hayes, David Porter, and Steve Cropper, collaborated with Otis Redding, Sam and Dave, Wilson Pickett, and others to record some of the grittiest but most graceful popular music ever created. At Hi, in the early 1970s, Al Green produced a series of unforgettable, deeply romantic recordings drenched in sensuality. At the beginning of the 1960s, Motown in Detroit had already begun to turn out an elegant version of soul that produced hit after crossover hit throughout the decade. Philadelphia, Chicago, New Orleans, and Los Angeles were just a few of the other important stops on the inspirational soul train in the 1960s and '70s.

For hippies the essential destination was San Francisco. There novelist Ken Kesey and his group of Merry Pranksters had used light shows accompanied by the music of the Grateful Dead to act as tour guides on LSD-fueled psychedelic trips for those who submitted to the Acid Test.

Kesey, like Harvard University professor Timothy Leary, was a proselytizer of what he saw as the transcendent experience to be had by using LSD and other hallucinogens. By the late 1960s LSD and the psychedelic music influenced by it seemed to be everywhere, including England, where the turned-on Beatles created their psychedelic-tinged masterpiece *Sgt. Pepper's Lonely Hearts Club* and where Pink Floyd's experiments with hallucinogens and psychedelia went into "interstellar overdrive." In Los Angeles, Jim Morrison, front man for the Doors, developed a reputation as a psychedelic shaman before the Dionysian excess of his drug and alcohol use ended his life (as it would those of rock's most virtuosic guitarist, Jimi Hendrix, and its most soulful white blues singer, Janis Joplin). Still, San Francisco remained the centre of the paisley-patterned, Day-Glo psychedelic universe with its ballroom venues, free-form radio, and a roster of extraordinary hometown bands that included the Grateful Dead, Jefferson Airplane, and Big Brother and the Holding Company. Across the country, in New York City, under the watchful eye of pop artist Andy Warhol and the influence of amphetamines and heroin, the Velvet Underground created a very different kind of experimental music that had limited commercial appeal for contemporary record buyers but that would be hugely influential to rock's future development.

The counterculture of the 1960s was never more prominently on display than at the outdoor festival concerts that became some of its signature events. Joplin and Otis Redding broke through to mass audiences at the Monterey Pop Festival in California in 1967, and Dylan deepened his ever-growing myth with his performance at England's Isle of Wight Pop Festival in 1969. The era's two most famous festivals, however, were the Woodstock Music and Arts Fair in rural upstate New York in August 1969, and the Altamont festival on the site of a racetrack in California in December of the same year. At Woodstock some 400,000 mostly young people successfully gathered for "three days of peace and music" despite inclement weather and a shortage of food and facilities for the crowd that was monumentally larger than expected. Some saw Woodstock as the dawn of a new age, others as its apotheosis, and still others as the beginning of its end. Surely the optimism of Woodstock nation was betrayed by the violence that erupted at Altamont, where the killing of an audience member was the ultimate result of the Rolling Stones' decision to allow the Hell's Angels motorcycle gang act as the festival's security force. For many Altamont served as the symbolic end of the rebellious hope and idealism of the 1960s.

You, on the other hand, are just at the beginning of this book's exploration of this extraordinary period. It can be a Rosetta Stone for decoding McLean's "American Pie" as it takes you on a magic carpet ride through the history of popular culture. Tune in, turn on your mind, relax, float downstream, and let the sound take you away.

CHAPTER 1

Rockin' in the U.K.

Rock musicians' pursuit of the new and innovative can be linked to the central sociological characteristic of rock music, its association with youth. In the 1950s and early 1960s it was a simple market equation: rock and roll was played by young musicians for young audiences and addressed young people's interests (quick sex and puppy love). It was therefore dismissed by many in the music industry as a passing novelty, "bubblegum," akin to the yo-yo or the hula hoop. But by the mid-1960s youth had become an ideological category that referred to a particular kind of hedonism, individualism, and modernism. Whereas youth once referred to high school students, it had come to include college students as well. Moreover, rock became multifunctional—dance and party music on the one hand, a matter of serious attention and intimate expression on the other. As rock spread globally this had different implications in different countries, but in general it allowed rock to continue to define itself as youthful even as its performers and listeners grew up and settled down. And it meant that rock's radical claim—the suggestion that the music remained somehow against the establishment even as it became part of it—was sustained by an adolescent irresponsibility, a commitment to the immediate thrills of sex 'n' drugs 'n' outrage and never mind the consequences.

BACKSTORY

Musically, rock is an eclectic hybrid that does not so much influence other types of music as colonize them, blurring musical boundaries. Its roots are in the styles of American music known as blues, rhythm and blues, and country music, all of which were outside the mainstream of popular music in the early 1950s and played only on small radio stations. In 1953, Alan Freed, a disc jockey in Cleveland, Ohio, began a program of rhythm and blues, then played only to black audiences. Drawing many listeners, it gave currency to the term he had adopted (though not invented) for the music, *rock and roll*. In the resulting form that emerged in 1955–56 with the rise to fame of Chuck Berry, Bill Haley, Little Richard, Buddy Holly, and, particularly, Elvis Presley, a quick-tempo version of rhythm and blues expressed emotional urgency and enthusiasm, with lyrics that mirrored the concerns of a young audience. This rhythmic, sensual music struck a responsive chord with teenagers.

Rock historians tend to arrange rock's past into a recurring pattern of emergence, appropriation, and decline. Thus, rock and roll emerged in the mid-1950s only to be appropriated by big business (for example, Presley's move from the Memphis label Sun to the national corporation RCA) and to decline into teen pop; the Beatles then emerged in the mid-1960s at the front of a British Invasion that led young Americans back to rock and roll's roots. But this notion is misleading. One reason for the Beatles' astonishing popularity by the end of the 1960s was precisely that they did not distinguish between the "authenticity" of, say, Chuck Berry and the "artifice" of the Marvelettes.

THE EARLY BRITISH REACTION

In Britain, as in the rest of Europe, rock and roll had an immediate youth appeal—each country soon had its own Elvis Presley—but it made little impact on national music media, as broadcasting was still largely under state control. (The connection between rock and radio in the United Kingdom was still to come.) Local rock and rollers had to make the music onstage rather than on record. In the United Kingdom musicians followed the skiffle group model of the folk, jazz, and blues scenes, the only local sources of American music making. The Beatles were only one of many provincial British groups who from the late 1950s played American music for their friends, imitating all kinds of hit sounds—from Berry to the Shirelles, from Carl Perkins to the Isley Brothers—while using the basic skiffle format of rhythm section, guitar, and shouting to be heard in cheap, claustrophobic pubs and youth clubs.

SKIFFLE

First popularized in the United States in the 1920s, skiffle was revived by British musicians in the mid-1950s. The term was originally applied to music played by jug bands (in addition to jugs, these bands featured guitars, banjos, harmonicas, and kazoos), first in Louisville, Kentucky, as early as 1905 and then more prominently in Memphis, Tennessee, in the 1920s and '30s.

In the Britain of the impoverished post-World War II years, young musicians were delighted to discover a style that could be played on a cheap guitar, a washboard scraped with thimbles, and a tea-chest bass (a broom handle and string attached

Lonnie Donegan with his band. Popperfoto/Getty Images

to a wooden case used for exporting tea). Leadbelly and Woody Guthrie were the heroes of a movement that had one foot in the blues and the other in folk music. When singer-banjoist Lonnie Donegan stepped out of the rhythm section of Chris Barber's Dixieland (traditional jazz) band to record a hopped-up version of Leadbelly's "Rock Island Line" in 1954, he was unwittingly laying the foundation of the 1960s British music scene. Released as a single in 1956, "Rock Island Line" was purchased by millions, including John Lennon and Paul McCartney of later Beatles fame, who thereby received their first exposure to African American popular music. Lennon and McCartney were among thousands of British boys who, inspired by Donegan, formed skiffle groups—in their case, the Quarrymen—as a first step on the road to rock and roll.

By 1962, encouraged by the anyone-can-play populism of skiffle and self-schooled in the music of Berry, Presley, Holly, Little Richard, Eddie Cochran, James Brown, and Muddy Waters, some British teens had a real feel for the rock-and-roll idiom. Blending that with such local traditions as dancehall, pop, and Celtic folk, they formulated original music they could claim, play, and sing with conviction. Young groups with electric guitars began performing and writing up-tempo melodic pop, fiery rock and roll, and Chicago-style electric blues.

In this context a group's most important instruments were their voices—on the one hand, individual singers (such as Lennon and McCartney) developed a new harshness and attack; on the other hand, group voices (vocal harmonies) had to do the decorative work provided on the original records by producers in the studio. Either way, it was through their voices that British beat groups, covering the same songs with the same lineup of instruments, marked themselves off from each other.

THE BEAT BOOM

Liverpool became the first hotbed of the so-called "beat boom." In the early 1960s it was unique among British cities in having more than 200 active pop groups. Many played youth clubs in the suburbs, but some made the big time in cellar clubs such as the Cavern (on Mathew Street) and the Jacaranda and the Blue Angel (on opposite sides of Steel Street) in the centre of the city. Previously these clubs had featured New Orleans-style traditional jazz bands and skiffle groups, but their repertoire changed to highlight American rhythm-and-blues hits, some of which sailors brought into the still active port; they were played by groups featuring electric guitar, bass, and drums.

Rory Storm and the Hurricanes, the Big Three, and the Beatles were top of the pile during 1960–61, but the Beatles acquired a special mystique after a couple of trips to Hamburg, West Germany, where club owners required them to play an extensive and varied repertoire for hours on end. The Cavern's manager, Allan Williams, booked the Beatles for a residency that led to their discovery by local department store manager Brian Epstein, who became their manager and orchestrated a national media campaign on behalf of Merseybeat (so named for the estuary that runs alongside Liverpool) artists. The Beatles first reached the British record charts in late 1962 (shortly after the Tornados' "Telstar," an instrumental smash that sent word of what was in store by becoming the first British record to top the American singles chart). Other exuberant Merseybeat male quartets—such as the Searchers, the Fourmost, and Gerry and the Pacemakers, plus the quintet Billy J. Kramer and the Dakotas—joined the hit parade in 1963.

Rock swept Britain. By 1964 Greater London could claim the Rolling Stones, the Yardbirds, the Who, the Kinks, the Pretty Things, Dusty Springfield, the Dave Clark Five, Peter and Gordon, Chad and Jeremy, and Manfred Mann. Manchester had the Hollies, Wayne Fontana and the Mindbenders, Freddie and the Dreamers, and Herman's Hermits. Newcastle had the Animals. And Birmingham had the Spencer Davis Group (featuring Steve Winwood) and the Moody Blues. Bands sprang up from Belfast (Them, with Van Morrison) to St. Albans (the Zombies), with more inventive artists arriving to keep the styles moving forward, including the Small Faces, the Move, the Creation, the Troggs, Donovan, the Walker Brothers, and John's Children.

BRITISH BLUES

In the early to mid-1960s another British musical movement developed that had more than a little overlap with the beat boom. Based in London clubs, British blues became an important influence on the subsequent rock explosion. Its founding fathers included guitarist Alexis Korner (born April 19, 1928, Paris, France—died January 1, 1984, London, England) and harmonica player Cyril Davies (born 1932, Denham, Buckinghamshire, England—died January 7, 1964, England), who played together in Blues Incorporated and passed on the influence of such heroes of Chicago's urban electric blues as Muddy Waters and Howlin' Wolf to a generation of younger musicians.

If it is possible to be both a midwife and a father figure, Alexis

5

THE YARDBIRDS

The early repertoire of the Yardbirds, who produced three of Britain's most influential rock guitarists, consisted almost exclusively of cover versions of songs by artists who recorded for the Chess and Vee Jay record labels. The original members were vocalist-harmonica player Keith Relf (born March 22, 1943, Richmond, Surrey, England—died May 14, 1976, London), guitarist Eric Clapton (born Eric Patrick Clapp, March 30, 1945, Ripley, Surrey), guitarist-bassist Chris Dreja (born November 11, 1946, London), drummer Jim McCarty (born July 25, 1943, Liverpool), bassist Paul Samwell-Smith (born May 8, 1943, London), and guitarist Anthony ("Top") Topham (born, England). Later members were guitarist Jeff Beck (born June 24, 1944, Wallington, Surrey) and guitarist Jimmy Page (born January 9, 1944, Heston, Middlesex).

With Clapton as lead guitarist, the band created the "rave-up," accelerating their playing until it transformed into white noise. Employing distortion and reverb (a succession of echoes that blend into one another to create sonic space), Clapton's successor, Beck, pushed later hits like "Shapes of Things" (1966) into the realm of psychedelic rock. Page, later the leader of one of the most successful heavy metal–hard rock groups of the 1970s, Led Zeppelin, initially joined the Yardbirds as a replacement for bassist Samwell-Smith. Switching to guitar, Page joined Beck as the band's colead guitarist—though the two played together on only one single, the visionary "Happenings Ten Years Time Ago" (1966), before the band's short-lived final lineup dissolved in 1968.

Korner played both roles for British rhythm and blues in 1962. He opened the Ealing Blues Club in a basement on Ealing Broadway and encouraged, inspired, and employed a number of musicians in his band,

Blues Incorporated, some of whom went on to form the Rolling Stones, Manfred Mann, and the Cyril Davies All-Stars. The Stones launched their career with a residency lasting several months during 1963 at the Crawdaddy Club, operated by promoter Georgio Gomelsky at the Station Hotel in respectable Richmond upon Thames, London. When the Stones left on a national tour to promote their first single, the Yardbirds, featuring guitar prodigy Eric Clapton, took their place at the Crawdaddy. Other suburban rhythm-and-blues and blues venues included the Railway Hotel in Harrow and the Caves at Chislehurst in Kent.

In central London deejay Guy Stevens played the latest American rhythm-and-blues and soul records at the Scene near Oxford Circus, and the Marquee and the 100 Club featured jazz bands in basements on opposite sides of Oxford Street. In 1964 the Marquee moved halfway down Wardour Street, where its new identity as London's base for blues-oriented rock was cemented by Clapton's successive appearances with the Yardbirds, John Mayall's Bluesbreakers, and Cream. Mayall's Bluesbreakers and Peter Green's Fleetwood Mac pleased their audiences by following a stricter agenda, modeling their music on the legendary guitarists B.B. King, Albert King,

and Freddie King (who shared the same last name but are unrelated).

As a self-contained form, British blues ended when Jimi Hendrix arrived from the United States to show local musicians the folly of their purist attitudes. Nevertheless, its legacy survived and flourished in the growing international heavy metal movement, a style built largely on a simplification of the loud, distorted riffing of the British blues guitarists. Clapton took the ideal of authentic performance from the British jazz scene, but his pursuit of originality—his homage to the blues originals and his search for his own guitar voice—also reflected his art-school education.

By the end of the 1960s, it was assumed that British rock groups wrote their own songs. What had once been a matter of necessity—there was a limit to the success of bands that played strictly cover versions, and Britain's professional songwriters had little understanding of these new forms of music—was now a matter of principle: self-expression onstage and in the studio was what distinguished these "rock" acts from pop "puppets" like Cliff Richard. (Groomed as Britain's Elvis Presley in the 1950s—moving with his band, the Shadows, from skiffle clubs to television teen variety shows—Richard was by the end of the 1960s a family

JOHN MAYALL

Singer, pianist, organist, and occasional guitarist John Mayall (born November 29, 1933, Macclesfield, Cheshire, England) was always a popular performer, but he was more celebrated for the musicians he attracted into his band, the Bluesbreakers. Through his patronage of several important guitarists, notably Eric Clapton, Peter Green, and Mick Taylor, he exerted an indirect but considerable influence on the course of rock music. Older by 10 years than most of his colleagues, Mayall was a canny operator whose devoted admirers cherished their hero's rugged individuality and anticommercial stance. However, his musical instincts were far from hidebound, as could be seen from the number of musicians who passed through his ranks on their way toward forming such groups as Cream (Clapton, Jack Bruce), Fleetwood Mac (Green, John McVie, Mick Fleetwood), Colosseum (Jon Hiseman, Dick Heckstall-Smith), and Free (Andy Fraser). Encouraged by his growing popularity in the United States, he moved to Los Angeles in the late 1960s and continued to lead a succession of bands featuring his own rough but effective singing.

entertainer, his performing style and material hardly even marked by rock and roll.)

ROCK ON RADIO AND TELEVISION IN THE U.K.

Until 1964, almost a decade after Bill Haley's "Rock Around the Clock" had introduced a new musical era to British youth, pop music fans found few stations to set their dial to. Indeed, the evenings-only English-language broadcasts from Radio Luxembourg—208 on the dial and transmitted from the grand duchy—represented the only pop music radio regularly available to British fans. Although the station's policy of leasing airtime to record companies meant having to hear a sequence of forgettable records on, for example, the Oriole label, there were unmissable treats, such as the American Top 20 on Sunday nights, which featured records that would not be released in the United Kingdom for weeks or even months—and that, even when released, might not be aired. Several stalwarts of British radio made their reputations at the station, including Barry Alldis, Paul Burnett, Noel Edmonds, David Jensen, and Jimmy Savile, who went from Radio Luxembourg to television's *Top of the Pops*. Perhaps the name most inextricably linked with the station is that of association football pools forecaster Horace Batchelor, whose Keynsham address—"that's K-E-Y-N-S-H-A-M"—was immortalized as the title of a Bonzo Dog Band album in 1969.

Before the advent of the British Broadcasting Corporation's (BBC's) pop network, Radio 1, coverage of pop music was all but confined to two weekend morning shows on the Light Programme network: *Saturday Club* and Sunday's *Easy Beat*. Both were presided over by Brian Matthew with the avuncular benevolence of an affable schoolteacher overseeing a lunchtime record hop. Hamstrung by "needle time" agreements that restricted the number of records the BBC could play, Matthew was hardly a disc jockey, given that those agreements meant that most of the music he introduced consisted of live cover versions of the records the listeners would have preferred to hear.

He also embraced each touted alternative to rock and roll, most notably skiffle—*Saturday Club* was originally called *Saturday Skiffle Club*—and the "trad jazz" (ersatz traditional New Orleans jazz) revival of the late 1950s, with an enthusiasm that aligned him with an older generation of listeners.

In 1961 Australian Alan ("Fluff") Freeman left Radio Luxembourg to join the BBC as the host of *Records Around Five*, where his trademark "At the Sign of the Swinging Cymbal" theme was first heard. Within months he moved to a new chart show, *Pick of the Pops*. Rescheduled in 1962 from Saturdays to a Sunday afternoon slot, *Pick of the Pops* became a pop radio institution, which Freeman, with his catchphrase opening, "Greetings, pop pickers," hosted for the next 10 years.

On Easter, 1964, Radio Caroline began broadcasting from a ship anchored in international waters off the coast of Essex in southeastern England. Moves to outlaw the station were under way within a week. But by the time Radio London, a station with a slickly professional sound and commercial clout, opened in December, the airwaves of the United Kingdom were cluttered with unlicensed broadcasters operating from either ships or disused marine defense emplacements. Audience figures grew

ISLAND RECORDS

Chris Blackwell grew up in Jamaica but was educated in England. He founded Island Records in 1959 in Jamaica, then three years later relocated to the United Kingdom, where Island became an outlet for Jamaican records, initially aimed at immigrant communities throughout Britain. In 1964, still without the distribution capability to hit the pop charts, Blackwell licensed his more commercial projects to Philips Records, including his production of "My Boy Lollipop" by Millie Small, which became the first international hit with the distinctive back-to-front beat of Jamaican ska music, and a string of hits by the Spencer Davis Group, the Birmingham band whose teenage organ player, Stevie Winwood, had one of the most distinctive voices of the era.

In 1967 Blackwell and his partner David Betteridge relocated Island to the bohemian surroundings of London's Notting Hill and redirected the company's focus toward the emerging rock audience, signing album-oriented acts with a college-based market. Winwood's new group, Traffic, became the flagship artist on Island's new pink label, and the American producer Joe Boyd helped to create a new genre of British folk rock with his productions of Fairport Convention and Nick Drake. In order to make Island's new direction clear, most Jamaican acts were released on various labels marketed by Trojan Records, run from separate premises under the supervision of Lee Gopthal. During the early 1970s Free and Roxy Music confirmed Island's position as the preeminent British independent label, and this gave Blackwell the confidence to support Bob Marley and the Wailers as album artists and to carry the music of Jamaica to a worldwide rock audience.

through 1965 as listeners embraced the formula of young, flamboyant disc jockeys and jingles and station identifications imported from the United States, punctuating a Top 40 playlist impervious to the "needle time" agreements between the BBC and record companies. It was not until July 1966, however, that the Marine Broadcasting (Offences) Bill began the parliamentary process that would outlaw offshore radio on August 15, 1967. By then the BBC's new Radio 1—with ex-pirate disc jockeys such as John Peel, Kenny Everett, and Tony Blackburn playing Top 40 hits peppered with American-made jingles—was only six weeks from its launch, and only Caroline among the major players risked prosecution, remaining on the air until March 1968.

The son of a tugboat captain, Kenny Everett (born Maurice James Christopher Cole) grew up in the suburbs of Liverpool. Following a brief period at seminary school, he worked in the advertising department of a shipping publication. He also made "air-check" style audition tapes, which he sent to the BBC and to Radio London, the slickest of the pirate radio stations anchored along the coastline of the United Kingdom in the mid-1960s. Upon being hired by Radio London, he changed his name (a legal precaution undertaken by most of the station's disc jockeys) to Kenny Everett.

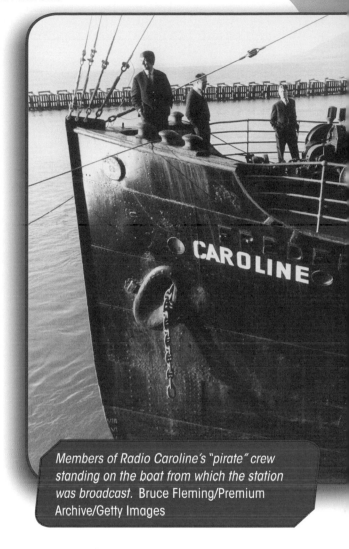

Members of Radio Caroline's "pirate" crew standing on the boat from which the station was broadcast. Bruce Fleming/Premium Archive/Getty Images

A sometimes surreal sense of humour that was much indebted to the Beatles and to *The Goon Show*, the influential British radio comedy of the 1950s that starred Peter Sellers, Spike Milligan, and Harry Secombe, soon established Everett as one of the outstanding personalities of pirate radio. When in 1967 the BBC launched Radio 1, the first land-based British pop station, Everett became one of its original recruits. His famed sense of humour resulted, however, in the end of his career as a live broadcaster on Radio 1 when in 1970, in response to a news item, he suggested that the wife of the transport minister had passed her driving test by bribing the examiner.

Radio unquestionably played a pivotal role in the spread of rock and roll in Britain, but as the 1960s unfolded television also became intimately involved. In February 1963 the Beatles appeared on Independent Television's (ITV's) *Thank Your Lucky Stars* (hosted by Brian Matthew), followed in July by the Rolling Stones. However, it was ITV's *Ready Steady Go!*, launched that August, and the BBC's *Top of the Pops*, which debuted in January 1964, that became essential weekly viewing for hip and not-so-hip fans alike. It was no coincidence that *Ready Steady Go!*'s life span—by the end of 1966 it was all over—precisely matched that of the mod era of youth-oriented fashion and consumerism; the show relayed "Swinging London's" music, style, and attitude to the rest of the country with minimum delay and maximum excitement, and it was arguably the most memorable "televisation" of the pop experience. *Top of the Pops* was more predictable, reflecting what British record buyers were already listening to, and continued to survive, with an essentially unaltered format.

CHAPTER 2

The Beatles

The Beatles began the 1960s as the biggest beat group in Liverpool, but within just a few years they had become the vehicle for the hopes and dreams of a generation that came of age in the 1960s. The famous quartet comprised Paul McCartney (in full Sir James Paul McCartney, born June 18, 1942, Liverpool, Merseyside, England), John Lennon (born October 9, 1940, Liverpool—died December 8, 1980, New York, New York, U.S.), George Harrison (born February 25, 1943, Liverpool—died November 29, 2001, Los Angeles, California), and Ringo Starr (born Richard Starkey, July 7, 1940, Liverpool). Other early members included Stuart Sutcliffe (born June 23, 1940, Edinburgh, Scotland—died April 10, 1962, Hamburg, West Germany [now Germany]) and Pete Best (born November 24, 1941, Madras [now Chennai], India).

COMING TOGETHER

Formed around the nucleus of Lennon and McCartney, who first performed together in Liverpool in 1957, the group grew out of a shared enthusiasm for American rock and roll. Like most early rock-and-roll figures, Lennon, a guitarist and singer, and McCartney, a bassist and singer, were largely self-taught as musicians. Precocious composers, they gathered around themselves a changing cast of accompanists, adding

The Beatles posing on the set of Granada TV's Late Scene Extra in 1963. From left to right: Paul McCartney, Ringo Starr, John Lennon, and George Harrison. Hulton Archive/Getty Images

by the end of 1957 Harrison, a lead guitarist, and then, in 1960 for several formative months, Sutcliffe, a promising young painter who brought into the band a brooding sense of bohemian style. After dabbling in skiffle, a jaunty sort of folk music popular in Britain in the late 1950s, and assuming several different names (the Quarrymen, the Silver Beetles, and, finally, the Beatles), the band added a drummer, Best, and joined a small but booming "beat music" scene, first in Liverpool and then, during several long visits between 1960 and 1962, in Hamburg—another seaport full of sailors thirsty for American rock and roll as a backdrop for their whiskey and womanizing.

In autumn 1961 Brian Epstein, a local Liverpool record store manager, saw the band and fell in love. Unshakably convinced of their commercial potential, Epstein became their manager and proceeded to bombard the major British music companies with letters and tape recordings of the band, finally winning a contract with Parlophone, a subsidiary of the giant EMI group of music labels. The man in charge of their career at Parlophone was George Martin, a classically trained musician who from the start put his stamp on the Beatles, first by suggesting the band hire a more polished drummer (they chose Starr) and then by rearranging their second recorded song (and first big British hit), "Please Please Me," changing it from a slow dirge into an up-tempo romp.

WHEN THEY WERE FAB: BEATLEMANIA

Throughout the winter and into the spring of 1963, the Beatles continued their rise to fame in England by producing spirited recordings of original tunes and also by playing classic American rock and roll on a variety of BBC radio programs. In these months, fascination with the Beatles—at first confined to young British fans of popular music—breached the normal barriers of taste, class, and age, transforming their recordings and live performances into matters of widespread public comment. In the fall of that year, when they belatedly made a couple of appearances on British television, the evidence of popular frenzy prompted British newspapermen to coin a new word for the phenomenon: Beatlemania. In early 1964, after equally tumultuous appearances on American television, the same phenomenon erupted in the United States and provoked a so-called British Invasion of Beatles imitators from the United Kingdom.

Beatlemania was something new. Musicians performing in the 19th century certainly excited a frenzy—one thinks of Franz Liszt—but that was before the modern mass media created the possibility of collective frenzy. Later pop music idols, such as Michael Jackson in the mid-1980s, Garth Brooks in the 1990s, and Mariah Carey in the early 21st century, sold similarly large numbers of records without provoking anything approaching the hysteria caused by the Beatles. By the summer of 1964, when the Beatles appeared in *A Hard Day's Night*, a movie that dramatized the phenomenon of Beatlemania,

THE REEPERBAHN

As rock and roll made its way to continental Europe in the late 1950s, several nightclub owners in the red-light district of Hamburg—the Reeperbahn, named for the street that was its main artery—decided that the new music should supplant the jazz they had been featuring. British sailors had told Bruno Koschmider, owner of the Kaiserkeller, about the music scene in London, and after visiting England he decided to import some musicians, whom he christened the Jets. Their guitarist, Tony Sheridan, became the Reeperbahn's first rock star and was soon lured away by a rival club, the Top Ten. Undaunted, Koschmider took advantage of the direct ship route to Liverpool to bring over inexpensive talent from that city, including Gerry and the Pacemakers, the Swinging Blue Jeans, Billy J. Kramer, the Searchers, and, most famously, the Beatles, whose first recording was as Tony Sheridan's backing group on a single for the German Polydor label.

As other clubs along the street, including the Star-Club, which proved to be the longest lasting, began booking rock-and-roll bands, the Reeperbahn became a magnet for British groups, who were housed in slum apartments, fed amphetamines to keep them going, and made to play back-breaking schedules. Besides drugs, violence was rife in the clubs, and waiters carried blackjacks and tear-gas pistols, which were also issued to some bands. Exhausting though the work was, the seemingly endless sets transformed the groups into tight musical units.

Furthermore, there was a group of young German intellectuals called "Exis" (from existentialists) who began frequenting the clubs. The most prominent were artists Klaus Voorman and his girlfriend Astrid Kirchherr, who had an affair with the Beatles' Stu Sutcliffe, took the first photos of the band, and designed their famous haircuts. Several figures from this group of young people later were instrumental in the beginnings of German rock. The Reeperbahn continued to be a laboratory for British groups until the mid-1960s; at that point British bands were making enough money at home not to have to endure the horrible working conditions in the Reeperbahn, and German bands had become good enough for the crowds frequenting the clubs.

the band's effect was evident around the world as countless young people emulated the band members' characteristic long hair, flip humour, and whimsical displays of devil-may-care abandon.

The popular hubbub proved to be a spur, convincing Lennon and McCartney of their songwriting abilities and sparking an outpouring of creative experimentation all but unprecedented in the history of rock music, which until then had been widely regarded, with some justification, as essentially a genre for juveniles.

TOMORROW NEVER KNOWS

Between 1965 and 1967 the music of the Beatles rapidly changed and evolved, becoming ever more subtle, sophisticated, and varied. Their repertoire in these years ranged from the chamber pop ballad "Yesterday" and the enigmatic folk tune "Norwegian Wood" (both in 1965) to the hallucinatory hard rock song "Tomorrow Never Knows" (1966), with a lyric inspired by Timothy Leary's handbook *The Psychedelic Experience* (1964). It also included the carnivalesque soundscape of "Being for the Benefit of Mr. Kite!" (1967), which featured stream-of-consciousness lyrics by Lennon and a typically imaginative arrangement (by George Martin) built around randomly spliced-together snippets of recorded steam organs—a tour de force of technological legerdemain quite typical of the band's studio work in this era.

In 1966 the Beatles announced their retirement from public performing to concentrate on exploiting the full resources of the recording studio. A year later, in June 1967, this period of widely watched creative renewal was climaxed by the

Beatlemania affected adults and young people alike, and crowds, such as this one surrounding a car carrying the Beatles in Australia, frequently greeted the group wherever it went. Keystone/Hulton Archive/Getty Images

release of *Sgt. Pepper's Lonely Hearts Club Band*, an album avidly greeted by young people around the world as indisputable evidence not only of the band's genius but also of the era's utopian promise. More than a band of musicians, the Beatles had come to personify, certainly in the minds of millions of young listeners, the joys of a new counterculture of hedonism and uninhibited experimentation— with music and with new ways of life. (Various members of the band in these years flirted with mind-expanding drugs such as LSD and also with exotic spiritual exercises such as transcendental meditation, a technique taught to them by Maharishi Mahesh Yogi, a barnstorming guru from India.)

In those years the Beatles effectively reinvented the meaning of rock and roll as a cultural form. The American artists they admired and chose to emulate—Chuck Berry, Little Richard, Fats Domino, Elvis Presley, the Everly Brothers, Buddy Holly, the pioneering rock composers

A HARD DAY'S NIGHT

Released in 1964 at the height of Beatlemania, *A Hard Day's Night* traces a fictitious day in the life of the Beatles, who portray themselves as they travel to London and attempt to record a performance on television while evading fanatical teenage admirers. Film critic Rex Reed derisively referred to playwright Alun Owen's script of *A Hard Day's Night* as a "non-screenplay." Yet it is precisely the inspired anarchy of Owen's screenplay—so suited to the Beatles' personalties that they appear to be improvising—that distinguishes this landmark musical. Until *A Hard Day's Night*, rock-and-roll movies were tame, sanitized affairs designed to conform to an older audience's sense of morality. This seemingly unstructured look at the Beatles took the world by storm by proving that the lads from Liverpool were not only great musicians but also had an irreverent sense of humour that was compared to that of the Marx Brothers and of BBC Radio's *The Goon Show*. The Beatles got memorable support from character actor Wilfred Brambell as Paul's "clean old man" of a grumpy grandfather.

Although he was an American filmmaker, director Richard Lester employed a range of techniques that were being pioneered by European New Wave filmmakers, including extensive use of handheld cameras and jump-cut editing. Lester and the Beatles collaborated the following year on *Help!* (1965).

Jerry Leiber and Mike Stoller, the influential soul songwriter Smokey Robinson, and, after 1964, folksinger and topical songwriter Bob Dylan—became widely regarded as canonic sources of inspiration, offering "classical" models for aspiring younger rock musicians. At the same time, the original songs the Beatles wrote and recorded dramatically expanded the musical range and expressive scope of the genre they had inherited. Their close vocal harmonies, subtle arrangements, and clever production touches, combined with an elemental rhythm section anchored by Starr's no-nonsense drumming, created new standards of excellence and beauty in a form of music previously known for amateurism.

After 1968 and the eruption of student protest movements in countries as different as Mexico and France, the Beatles insensibly surrendered their role as de facto leaders of an inchoate global youth culture. They nevertheless continued for several more years to record and release new music and maintained a level of popularity rarely rivaled before or since. In 1968 they launched their own record label, Apple; hoping to nurture experimental pop art, they instead produced chaos and commercial failure, apart from the work of the Beatles themselves. The band continued to enjoy widespread popularity. The following year *Abbey Road* went on to become one of the band's best-loved and biggest-selling albums.

"I DON'T BELIEVE IN BEATLES"

Meanwhile, personal disagreements magnified by the stress of symbolizing the dreams of a generation had begun to tear the band apart. Once the collaborative heart and soul of the band, Lennon and McCartney fell into bickering and mutual accusations of ill will. By now millions of dollars were at stake, and the utopian aura of the performers was in jeopardy, given the discrepancy between the band's symbolic stature as idols of a carefree youth culture and their newfound real status as pampered plutocrats.

In the spring of 1970 the Beatles formally disbanded. In the years that followed, all four members went on to produce solo albums of variable quality and popularity. Lennon released a corrosive set of songs with his new wife, Yoko Ono, and McCartney went on to form a band, Wings, that turned out a fair number of commercially successful recordings in the 1970s. Starr and Harrison, too, initially had some success as solo artists. But, as time went by, the Beatles became as much of a historical curio as Al Jolson or Bing Crosby or Frank Sinatra or Elvis Presley before them.

In 1980 Lennon was murdered by a demented fan outside the Dakota, an apartment building in New York City known for its celebrity tenants. The event provoked a global outpouring of grief. Lennon is memorialized in Strawberry Fields, a section of Central Park across from the Dakota that Yoko Ono landscaped in her husband's honour.

ON THEIR OWN

In the years that followed, the surviving former Beatles continued to

A crowd gathers at Strawberry Fields in Central Park in New York City to remember John Lennon on the 30th anniversary of his death in 2010.
Jemal Countess/Getty Images

record and perform as solo artists. McCartney in particular remained musically active, both in the pop field, producing new albums every few years, and in the field of classical music—in 1991 he completed *Liverpool Oratorio*; in 1997 he supervised the recording of another symphonic work of large ambition, *Standing Stone*; and in 1999 he released a new classical album, *Working Classical*. McCartney was knighted by the queen of England in 1997. Starr was also very visible in the 1990s, touring annually with his All-Star Band, a rotating group of rock veterans playing their hits on the summertime concert circuit. Beginning in 1988, Harrison recorded with Bob Dylan, Tom Petty, Jeff Lynne, and Roy Orbison in a loose amalgam known as the Traveling Wilburys, but, for most of the 1980s and '90s, he had a low profile as a musician while acting as the producer of several successful films. After surviving a knife attack at his home in 1999, Harrison succumbed to a protracted battle with cancer in 2001.

REPRESENTATIVE WORKS

- ▶ "I Want to Hold Your Hand" (1963)
- ▶ "Please Please Me" (1963)
- ▶ "She Loves You" (1963)
- ▶ "Twist and Shout" (1963)
- ▶ *With the Beatles* (1963)
- ▶ "A Hard Day's Night" (1964)
- ▶ "I Feel Fine"/"She's a Woman" (1964)
- ▶ *Help!* (1965)
- ▶ *Rubber Soul* (1965)
- ▶ "Paperback Writer"/"Rain" (1966)
- ▶ *Revolver* (1966)
- ▶ *Sgt. Pepper's Lonely Hearts Club Band* (1967)
- ▶ "Strawberry Fields Forever"/"Penny Lane" (1967)
- ▶ *The Beatles* [*White Album*] (1968)
- ▶ "Hey Jude"/"Revolution" (1968)
- ▶ *Abbey Road* (1969)
- ▶ "Let It Be" (1970)

Early in the 1990s McCartney, Harrison, and Starr had joined to add harmonies to two previously unreleased vocal recordings by Lennon. These new songs by "the Beatles" served as a pretext for yet another publicity blitz, aimed at creating a market for a lavishly produced quasi-historical series of archival recordings assembled under the supervision of the band and released in 1995 and 1996 as *The Beatles Anthology*, a collection of six compact discs that supplemented a 10-hour-long authorized video documentary of the same name. A compilation of the band's number one singles, *1*, appeared in 2000 and enjoyed worldwide success, topping the charts in such countries as England and the United States. The afterglow of Beatlemania may have disappeared, but the iconography of an era of youthful tumult had been reverently preserved for posterity.

The Beatles were inducted into the Rock and Roll Hall of Fame in 1988, and Lennon (1994), McCartney (1999), and Harrison (2004) were also inducted as solo performers. In September 2009, specially packaged digitally remastered versions of the Beatles' entire catalog and a Beatles version of the popular electronic music game *Rock Band* were released simultaneously. After it was reported in February 2010 that the financially troubled EMI was soliciting buyers for its Abbey Road Studios, where the Beatles made the great majority of their recordings, the British Department for Culture, Media, and Sport declared the recording complex a historic landmark. EMI subsequently announced that it would retain ownership of the iconic studio while seeking outside investment to improve its facilities.

CHAPTER 3

The Rolling Stones

In the 1960s the Rolling Stones were the yang to the Beatles' yin, at least in the popular press. Formed in 1962, the Stones drew on Chicago blues stylings to create a unique vision of the dark side of post-1960s counterculture. The original members were Mick Jagger (born July 26, 1943, Dartford, Kent, England), Keith Richards (born December 18, 1943, Dartford), Brian Jones (born February 28, 1942, Cheltenham, Gloucestershire—died July 3, 1969, Hartfield, Sussex), Bill Wyman (born October 24, 1936, London), and Charlie Watts (born June 2, 1941, London). Later members were Mick Taylor (born January 17, 1948, Hereford, East Hereford and Worcester), Ron Wood (born June 1, 1947, London), and Darryl Jones (born December 11, 1961, Chicago, Illinois, U.S.).

"THE GREATEST ROCK-AND-ROLL BAND IN THE WORLD"

No rock band has sustained consistent activity and global popularity for so long a period as the Rolling Stones, still capable, a half-century after their formation, of filling the largest stadia in the world. Though several of their mid-1960s contemporaries—notably Bob Dylan, Paul McCartney, Eric Clapton, and Van Morrison—have maintained individual positions in rock's front line, the Rolling Stones' nucleus of

The original lineup of the Rolling Stones in 1964. From left to right: Bill Wyman, Mick Jagger, Brian Jones, Charlie Watts, and Keith Richards. GAB Archive/Redferns/Getty Images

singer Jagger, guitarist Richards, and drummer Watts remains rock's most durable ongoing partnership.

In the process, the Stones have become rock's definitive, emblematic band: a seamless blend of sound, look, and public image. It may be debatable whether they have actually, at any given moment, been the "greatest rock-and-roll band in the world," as their time-honoured onstage introduction has claimed them to be; that they are the mold from which various generations of challengers—from the Who, Led Zeppelin, and Aerosmith via the New York Dolls, the Clash, and the Sex Pistols all the way to Guns N' Roses, U2, Oasis, and Coldplay—have been struck is not. In their onstage personae, Jagger and Richards established the classic rock band archetypes: the preening, narcissistic singer and the haggard, obsessive guitarist.

ENGLAND'S NEWEST HIT MAKERS

Formed in London as an alliance between Jagger, Richards, and multi-instrumentalist Brian Jones along with Watts and bassist Wyman, the Stones began as a grubby conclave of students and bohemians playing a then-esoteric music based on Chicago ghetto blues in pubs and clubs in and around West London. Their potential for mass-market success seemed negligible at first, but by 1965 they were second only to the Beatles in the collective affection of teenage Britain. However, whereas the Beatles of the mid-1960s had longish hair, wore matching suits, and appeared utterly charming, the Stones had considerably longer hair, all dressed differently, and seemed thoroughly intimidating. As the Beatles grew ever more respectable and reassuring, the Stones became correspondingly more rebellious and threatening. The Stones—specifically Jagger, Richards, and Jones—were subjected to intense police and press harassment for drug use and all-purpose degeneracy, whereas the Beatles, who were in private life no less fond of marijuana, sex, and alcohol, were welcomed at Buckingham Palace and made Members of the Order of the British Empire (M.B.E.) by the queen.

The Stones' early repertoire consisted primarily of recycled gems from the catalogs of the blues and rock-and-roll titans of the 1950s: their first five singles and the bulk of their first two albums were composed by others. The turning point was reached when, spurred on by the example of the Beatles' John Lennon and Paul McCartney, Jagger and Richards began composing their own songs, which not only ensured the long-term viability of the band but also served to place the Jagger-Richards team firmly in creative control of the group. Jones had been their prime motivating force in their early days, and he was the band's most gifted instrumentalist as well as its prettiest face, but he had little talent for composition and became increasingly marginalized. His textural wizardry dominated their first all-original album, *Aftermath* (1966), which featured him on marimba, dulcimer, sitar, and assorted keyboards as well as on his customary guitar and harmonica. Thereafter, however, he declined in both creativity and influence, becoming a depressive, drug-sodden liability eventually fired by the band mere weeks before his death.

The Jagger-Richards songwriting team created its first bona fide classic, "(I Can't Get No) Satisfaction," in 1965 and enjoyed a string of innovative hit singles well into 1966, including "Paint It Black," "19th Nervous Breakdown," "Get Off of My Cloud," "Have You Seen Your Mother, Baby," and "Lady Jane," but the era of art-pop and psychedelia, which coincided with the Beatles' creative peak, represented a corresponding trough for the Stones. The fashions of the era of whimsy and flower power did not suit their essentially dark and disruptive energies, and their psychedelic album *Their Satanic Majesties Request* (1967), with its accompanying single "We Love You," was a comparatively feeble riposte to the Beatles' all-conquering *Sgt. Pepper's Lonely Hearts Club Band* and contributed little beyond its title to their legend. Furthermore, they were hampered by seemingly spending as much time in court and jail as they did in the studio or on tour. However, as the mood of the time darkened, the Stones hit a new stride in 1968 with the epochal single "Jumpin' Jack Flash," which reconnected them to their blues-rock roots, and the album *Beggars Banquet*. Replacing Jones with the virtuosic but self-effacing guitarist Mick Taylor, they returned to the road in 1969, almost instantly becoming rock's premier touring attraction.

EXILES ON MAIN STREET

By the end of 1970 the Beatles had broken up, Jimi Hendrix was dead, and Led Zeppelin had barely appeared on the horizon. Though Led Zeppelin eventually outsold the Stones by five albums to one, no group could challenge their central position in the rock pantheon. Moreover, the death of Brian Jones combined with Taylor's lack of onstage presence elevated public perception of Richards's status from that of Jagger's right-hand man to effective coleader of the band.

The period between "Jumpin' Jack Flash" and the double album *Exile on Main Street* (1972) remains their creative and iconic peak. Including

THE ALTAMONT FESTIVAL

As the final show of their American tour, the Rolling Stones held a one-day rock festival at Altamont Speedway in Livermore, California, on December 6, 1969. The free event was intended as a thank-you gesture by the band to their fans and was to feature Santana; the Jefferson Airplane; the Flying Burrito Brothers; Crosby, Stills and Nash; and the Rolling Stones themselves. The most notable flaw of the haphazardly organized festival (besides its relatively inaccessible location) was the hiring of the Oakland chapter of the Hell's Angels motorcycle gang as security, a shocking bit of naïveté on the band's part. Trouble started early on, when Marty Balin of the Jefferson Airplane was knocked down with an Angel's pool cue and a confused naked man was beaten to the ground. The disorder reached its climax during the Stones' appearance, when Meredith Hunter, an 18-year-old African American man, rushed the stage

The Rolling Stones' Mick Jagger (left) *and Keith Richards performing at the Altamont festival in Livermore, California, in 1969.* Robert Altman/ Michael Ochs Archives/Getty Images

with a gun and was stabbed to death before Mick Jagger's eyes. Much has been written about Altamont as "the day the '60s died" and "the anti-Woodstock," but, given the way most festivals were organized at the time, violence at a festival was perhaps inevitable.

the studio albums *Let It Bleed* (1969) and *Sticky Fingers* (1971) plus the in-concert *Get Yer Ya-Yas Out!* (1970), it gave them the repertoire and image that still defines them and on which they have continued to trade ever since: an incendiary blend of sex, drugs, Satanism, and radical politics delivered with their patented fusion of Jagger's ironic distance and Richards's tatterdemalion intensity. Their records and concerts at this time both explored and provided the soundtrack for the contradictions of a collapsing counterculture at a time when almost everybody else—the Doors, the Velvet Underground, and Frank Zappa's Mothers of Invention excepted—still seemed to be in a state of psychedelic euphoria.

Produced first by Glyn Johns and Jimmy Miller and then by Jagger and Richards themselves (as the "Glimmer Twins"), their recordings of this period found them adding country music to their list of influences and—most notably on *Beggars Banquet*—adding more and more acoustic guitar textures to their already impressive command of musical light and shade. Yet their blues-powered foray into the era's heart of darkness bore bitter fruit indeed: when a young black man was murdered by Hell's Angels (hired as security) at a disastrous free concert at the Altamont Speedway in Livermore, California, during their 1969 American tour, it seemed to many observers that the Stones' own aura of decadence and danger was somehow to blame for the tragedy.

The quality of their music began to decline after *Exile on Main Street*. Jagger and Richards began to act out the group's fascination with the juxtaposition of high society and lowlife: the singer became a jet-set figure; the guitarist, a full-time junkie who finally "cleaned up" in 1977 and thereby saved both his own life and the band's future. Taylor left in 1975 to be replaced by Wood, formerly of the Faces, and, despite the occasional

REPRESENTATIVE WORKS

- ▶ "It's All Over Now" (1964)
- ▶ "The Last Time" (1965)
- ▶ "(I Can't Get No) Satisfaction" (1965)
- ▶ *Beggars Banquet* (1968)
- ▶ "Jumpin' Jack Flash" (1968)
- ▶ "Street Fighting Man" (1968)
- ▶ "Honky Tonk Woman" (1969)
- ▶ *Let It Bleed* (1969)
- ▶ *Get Yer Ya-Yas Out!* (1970)
- ▶ "Brown Sugar" (1971)
- ▶ *Sticky Fingers* (1971)
- ▶ *Exile on Main Street* (1972)
- ▶ *Hot Rocks 1964–71* (1972)
- ▶ "It's Only Rock'n'Roll" (1974)
- ▶ "Miss You" (1978)
- ▶ "Emotional Rescue" (1980)
- ▶ "Start Me Up" (1981)
- ▶ "Undercover of the Night" (1983)
- ▶ *Jump Back: The Best of the Rolling Stones 1971–1993* (1993)

bright spot like *Some Girls* (1978), *Emotional Rescue* (1980), or "Start Me Up" (1981), the Stones' albums and singles became increasingly predictable, though their tours continued to sell out. They even briefly disbanded in the late 1980s after a public spat between Jagger and Richards. Both leaders recorded solo albums that performed relatively poorly in the marketplace, though Richards's work was significantly more favourably reviewed than Jagger's.

Disputes settled, the Stones reconvened in 1989 for their *Steel Wheels* album and tour. Wyman retired in 1992 and was replaced on tour by Daryl Jones, formerly a bassist for Miles Davis and Sting, and in the studio by a variety of guest musicians. Jagger, Richards, Watts, and Wood continue to trade as the Rolling Stones, and, whenever they tour, audiences flock in the thousands to discover if the old lions can still roar. The general consensus is that they can. In their late middle age the ultimate rebels became the ultimate institution, and to many they remain the ultimate rock band.

Several prominent directors have sought to translate the electricity of the Stones as live performers to the screen, including Jean-Luc Godard, with the impressionistic *Sympathy for the Devil* (1968); Hal Ashby, with *Let's Spend the Night Together* (1982); and, perhaps most notably, David Maysles, Albert Maysles, and Charlotte Zwerin, with *Gimme Shelter* (1970), which covered the group's 1969 tour and Altamont Speedway concert. More recently, in the wake of the group's well-received album *A Bigger Bang* (2005), director Martin Scorsese, long a fan of the group, focused less on the spectacle of a Stones' concert and more on the band as performers. The result, *Shine a Light* (2008), met with critical acclaim and confirmed that the Rolling Stones are still a major presence in the rock scene of the 21st century.

CHAPTER 4

British Invasion

While the beat boom provided Britons relief from the postimperial humiliation of hand-me-down rock, the Beatles and their ilk brought the United States more than credible simulations. They arrived as foreign ambassadors, with distinctive accents (in conversation only; most of the groups sang in "American"), slang, fashions, and personalities. The Beatles' first film, *A Hard Day's Night* (1964), further painted England as the centre of the (rock) universe. American media took the bait and made Carnaby Street, London's trendy fashion centre in the 1960s, a household name.

The Beatles' triumphant arrival in New York City on February 7, 1964, opened America's doors to a wealth of British musical talent. What followed would be called—with historical condescension by the willingly reconquered colony—the second British Invasion. From 1964 to 1966 the United Kingdom sent a stream of hits across the Atlantic. Behind the conquering Beatles, Peter and Gordon ("A World Without Love"), the Animals ("House of the Rising Sun"), Manfred Mann ("Do Wah Diddy Diddy"), Petula Clark ("Downtown"), Freddie and the Dreamers ("I'm Telling You Now"), Wayne Fontana and the Mindbenders ("Game of Love"), Herman's Hermits ("Mrs. Brown You've Got a Lovely Daughter"), the Rolling Stones ("[I Can't Get No] Satisfaction" and others), the Troggs ("Wild Thing"), and Donovan ("Sunshine Superman") all topped Billboard's singles chart. These charming invaders had borrowed (often literally) American rock music and returned it—restyled and refreshed—to a generation largely ignorant of its historical and racial origins.

In April 1966 *Time* magazine effectively raised the white flag with a cover story on "London: The Swinging City." Peace quickly followed; by the pivotal year 1967 a proliferation of English and American bands were equal partners in one international rock culture.

THE ANIMALS

From northeastern England, the Animals were a five-piece rock group whose driving sound influenced Bob Dylan's decision, in 1965, to begin working with musicians playing electric instruments. The principal members were Eric Burdon (born May 11, 1941, Newcastle upon Tyne, Tyne and Wear, England), Alan Price (born April 19, 1942, Fatfield, Durham), Hilton Valentine (born May 21, 1943, North Shields, Tyne and Wear), Chas Chandler (born Bryan Chandler, December 18, 1938, Heaton, Tyne and Wear—died July 17, 1996), and John Steel (born February 4, 1941, Gateshead, Durham).

Released in 1964, the group's first single was a version of Eric Von Schmidt's folk-blues song "Baby Let Me Follow You Down," which had appeared on Dylan's first album.

Retitled "Baby Let Me Take You Home," it featured Burdon's hoarse rhythm-and-blues-inflected singing. Their second single, the traditional "House of the Rising Sun," was brilliantly rearranged to feature Price's electric organ and Valentine's guitar, playing ornate arpeggios beneath Burdon's dramatic vocal. A number one hit on both sides of the Atlantic, this was the record that persuaded Dylan to take the plunge into electric music. The group's later hits, such as "I'm Crying," "We Gotta Get Out of This Place," and "It's My Life," developed a formula of tough, dramatic, hard-driving rock shaped by an awareness of folk music and the blues, but the departure of Price in 1965 and Burdon a year later put a premature end to the story. Both pursued solo careers, whereas Chandler went on to manage Jimi Hendrix and Slade. The Animals were inducted into the Rock and Roll Hall of Fame in 1994.

THE KINKS

Formed as a rhythm-and-blues band in 1963 by brothers Ray and Dave Davies, the Kinks originated in Muswell Hill in northern London. By infusing their rhythm-and-blues beginnings with sharp social observation and the theatricality of the British music hall, the Kinks became an English archetype. The principal members were Ray

THE "FIFTH BEATLE"

When pioneering disc jockey Alan Freed fell from grace in 1958, Murray the K (Murray Kaufman) took his place as the main man on the rhythm-and-blues and rock-and-roll scene for New York City's popular WINS radio. Advised by American groups that had opened for the Beatles in Britain that Murray was the man to see in New York, the Beatles' manager, Brian Epstein, made sure that the deejay had plenty of access to the Fab Four when they made their first trip to the United States in 1964. Murray broadcast from the Beatles' hotel room, hosted their performance at Carnegie Hall, traveled with the group to their concerts in Washington, D.C., and Miami, and, later, even hosted a show by the band at London's Wembley Stadium. In the process George Harrison dubbed him the "Fifth Beatle."

Davies (born June 21, 1944, London, England), Dave Davies (born February 3, 1947, London), Peter Quaife (born December 31, 1943, Tavistock, Devonshire—died June 23, 2010, Herlev, Denmark), and Mick Avory (born February 15, 1944, London).

Built on power chords, their third single, "You Really Got Me," provided their big break. It stands, along with the work of the early Rolling Stones, as a landmark of creative exploration of rhythm and blues by white musicians. As such, it had a huge influence on the early Who, mid-1960s American garage punk, and early 1970s heavy metal. Moreover, the Kinks exaggerated the androgynous image cultivated by the Rolling Stones with foppish clothes, extremely long hair, and Ray Davies's often camp demeanour. After two more international hits, "All Day and All of the Night" and "Tired of Waiting for You," the Kinks quickly diversified their approach with the remarkable "See My Friends" (1965), an ambiguous story of male bonding, which represents the first satisfying fusion of Western pop with Indian

The Kinks performing. From left to right: Ray Davies, Pete Quaife, Mick Avory, and Dave Davies. David Redfern/Redferns/Getty Images

musical forms. As their impact on the American market lessened after a disastrous tour in 1965, the Kinks became more idiosyncratically English, with social comment songs like "A Well-Respected Man," "Dedicated Follower of Fashion," and "Sunny Afternoon," the last of which reached number one on the U.K. charts in 1966 and on which Ray Davies imitated 1930s British crooner Al Bowlly.

At once a satirist and romantic, Ray Davies combined a knack for writing sweet melodies with witty, empathetic lyrics and an instantly distinctive vocal delivery. With his wife, Rasa, and brother Dave providing the high backing vocals, Ray delivered a trio of classics in 1966–67: "Dead End Street," which addressed poverty during the final days of the 1960s economic boom; "Big Black Smoke," a cautionary tale about a teenage runaway; and "Waterloo Sunset," a hymn to London that became the Kinks' signature song. In 1967 Dave scored a solo success with "Death of a Clown," a memorable drinking song.

After 12 consecutive Top 20 singles in the United Kingdom, the Kinks started to slip in 1968 and spent the next two years attempting to rebuild their career in the United States by adapting to the new rock market with heavier instrumentation and elongated songs. They returned to the Top Ten on both sides of the Atlantic in 1970 with "Lola," the story of an encounter with a transvestite that capitalized on Ray's theatrical persona. Several years as a top concert attraction in the United States followed, but Ray's struggle to reverse bad business deals made in the early 1960s took its creative toll. After *Everybody's in Show-biz, Everybody's a Star* (1972), Ray Davies's isolation—once so charming—had become curmudgeonly.

Energized by the punk rock they had influenced, the Kinks returned to rock with album successes in the United States such as *Low Budget* (1979). "Come Dancing" (1983), inspired by Davies family history, was a hit in both the United Kingdom and the United States. Thereafter, despite the departure of all the original members except the Davies brothers, the Kinks (who were inducted into the Rock and Roll Hall of Fame in 1990) continued to record and perform, with Ray finding success with a one-man show based on his autobiography, *X-Ray* (1994).

THE WHO

Though primarily inspired by American rhythm and blues, the Who took a bold step toward defining a uniquely British rock vernacular in the 1960s. Shunning the Beatles' idealized romance and the Rolling Stones' cocky swagger, the Who shunned pretension and straightforwardly dealt with teenage travails. At a time when rock music was uniting young people all over the world, the Who were friendless, bitter outsiders.

The principal members were Pete Townshend (born May 19, 1945, London, England), Roger Daltrey (born March 1, 1944, London), John Entwistle (born October 9, 1944, London—died June 27, 2002, Las Vegas, Nevada, U.S.), and Keith Moon (born August 23, 1946, London— died September 7, 1978, London). Moon was replaced by Kenny Jones (born September 16, 1948, London). Townshend and Entwistle joined Daltrey in his group, the Detours, in 1962; with drummer Doug Sandom they became, in turn, the Who and the High Numbers. Moon replaced Sandom in early 1964, after which the group released a self-consciously mod single ("I'm the Face") to little notice and became the Who again in late 1964. The West London quartet cultivated a Pop art image to suit the fashion-obsessed British "mod" subculture and matched that look with the rhythm-and-blues sound that mod youth favoured. Townshend ultimately acknowledged that clothing made from the Union Jack, sharp suits, pointy boots, and short haircuts were a contrivance, but it did the trick, locking in a fanatically devoted core following. Fashion, however, was strictly a starting point for the

Who; by the late 1960s the mods were history, and the Who were long past needing to identify themselves with the uniform of any movement.

The band's early records dealt with alienation, uncertainty, and frustration, lashing out with tough lyrics, savage power chords and squalling feedback by guitarist-songwriter Townshend, the kinetic assault of drummer Moon and bassist Entwistle, and the macho brawn of singer Daltrey. The four singles that introduced the Who between January 1965 and March 1966—"I Can't Explain," "Anyway, Anyhow, Anywhere," "My Generation," and "Substitute"—declared themselves in an unprecedented fury of compressed sonic aggression, an artistic statement matched and intensified onstage by Townshend's habit of smashing his guitar to climax concerts. While other groups were moving toward peace-and-love idealism, the Who sang of unrequited lust ("Pictures of Lily"), peer pressure ("Happy Jack"), creepy insects (Entwistle's "Boris the Spider"), and gender confusion ("I'm a Boy"). As one instrument after another ended in splinters, the Who firmly declared themselves proponents of making violent rage a form of rock catharsis.

Until the 1967 release of *The Who Sell Out*, a sardonic concept album presented as a pirate radio broadcast, the Who were primarily a singles group. They were, however, more successful in this regard in Britain (eight Top Ten hits between 1965 and 1967) than in the United States ("I Can See for Miles," released in 1967, was the group's only Billboard Top Ten single). It was the 1969 rock opera *Tommy*—and a memorable performance at Woodstock that summer—that made the Who a world-class album-rock act. In the process, Townshend was recognized as one of rock's most intelligent, articulate, and self-conscious composers.

The Who cemented their standing with *Who's Next* (1971), an album of would-be teen anthems ("Won't Get Fooled Again," "Baba O'Riley") and sensitive romances ("Behind Blue Eyes," "Love Ain't for Keeping"), all reflecting Townshend's dedication to his "avatar," the Indian mystic Meher Baba. That same year, Entwistle released a solo album, the darkly amusing *Smash Your Head Against the Wall*; Townshend issued his first solo album, *Who Came First*, in 1972; and Daltrey offered his, *Daltrey*, in 1973. Still, the Who continued apace, releasing Townshend's second magnum rock opera, *Quadrophenia*, in 1973, *The Who by Numbers* in 1975, and *Who Are You* in 1978.

Moon ("the Loon"), whose excessive lifestyle was legendary, died of an accidental drug overdose in 1978 and was replaced by Jones (formerly of the Small Faces and the Faces). So constituted, the Who released *Face Dances* (1981) and *It's Hard* (1982) before disbanding in 1982. Daltrey pursued acting while letting his solo career taper off. Entwistle released occasional records to little effect. Townshend busied himself briefly as a book editor while undertaking a variety of solo ventures—from well-received Who-like rock records such as *Empty Glass* (1980) to *The Iron Man* (1989), a less-successful experiment in musical theatre that nevertheless paved the way for the triumphant delivery of *Tommy* to Broadway in 1993. Townshend, Daltrey, and Entwistle reunited for tours in 1989 and 1996–97. The Who was about to embark on a U.S. tour in 2002 when Entwistle died.

Tommy remains the Who's most enduring creation. On its way to the theatre, *Tommy* became an all-star orchestral album in 1972 and a garish film with Daltrey in the title role in 1975. *Quadrophenia* also was made into a film, in 1979, and was revived by the touring Who as a stagy rock spectacle in the 1990s.

In 2005 and 2006 Townshend serialized a novella, *The Boy Who Heard Music*, online, and a set of related songs constituted "Wire & Glass," the mini-opera that made up part of *Endless Wire* (2006), which was the first album of new Who material since 1982. On it Townshend and Daltrey were supported by drummer Zak Starkey (son of Ringo Starr) and Townshend's brother Simon on guitar, among others. A full-blown musical based on this material and also titled *The Boy Who Heard Music* premiered in July 2007 at Vassar College in Poughkeepsie, N.Y. A year later the Who were celebrated (and performed) at a VH1 Rock Honors concert. The Who was inducted into the Rock and Roll Hall of Fame in 1990.

THE HOLLIES

Like most of their contemporaries in the British beat boom, the Hollies, from Manchester, found their earliest influences in American rhythm-and-blues artists. The principal members were Allan Clarke (born April 15, 1942, Salford, Lancashire, England), Graham Nash (born February 2, 1942, Blackpool, Lancashire), Tony Hicks (born December 16, 1943, Nelson, Lancashire), Eric Haydock (born February 3, 1943, Burnley, Lancashire), Bernie Calvert (born September 16, 1943, Burnley), and Terry Sylvester (born January 8, 1947, Liverpool, Merseyside).

Their first hits in the United Kingdom, in 1963–64, were with cover versions of the Coasters' "(Ain't That) Just Like Me" and "Searchin'," Maurice Williams and the Zodiacs' "Stay," and Doris Troy's "Just One Look." Under the influence of Bob Dylan, however,

their approach broadened, including diluted elements of folk music, to the particular benefit of Clarke. A strong lead singer, he received fine support from the harmony singing of Hicks, Nash, and, after the latter's departure in 1968, Sylvester on "Here I Go Again" (1964), "I'm Alive" (1965), "Bus Stop" (1966, their first entry into the American Top Ten), and "He Ain't Heavy, He's My Brother" (1969). At their best the Hollies established a clear balance between the various components at play in their music, developing (like their Liverpool contemporaries the Searchers) a style that provided a useful template for a new generation of power pop groups, many of them American, such as the Raspberries and the Rubinoos. Unlike most groups of their vintage, the Hollies had their greatest successes in the 1970s, with "Long Cool Woman (in a Black Dress)" (1972) and "The Air That I Breathe" (1974). The group was inducted into the Rock and Roll Hall of Fame in 2010.

DUSTY SPRINGFIELD

The daughter of a tax consultant, Dusty Springfield (born Mary Isabel Catherine Bernadette O'Brien, April 16, 1939, London, England—died March 2, 1999, Henley-on-Thames, Oxfordshire) grew up in prosperous Hampstead in North London. After success in the early 1960s with her brother Tom in the British country-music trio the Springfields, she went solo and made her way into the heart of "Swinging London." Part cartoon, part unresolvable desire, part bruised despair, she peered through heavy mascara and a stack of peroxided hair while singing with breathy sensuality. Bringing a fragile uncertainty to her cover versions of songs by Burt Bacharach and Hal David that had been hits in the United States for Dionne Warwick, Springfield had a string of British hits. The high point of her career, though, was the ballad "You Don't Have to Say You Love Me" (1966), which reached number four on the American charts.

In the late 1960s she began to take herself seriously as a soul diva, signing with Atlantic Records and cutting her *Dusty in Memphis* (1969) album in the famed American Sound Studios with producers Jerry Wexler and Arif Mardin. It brought her an international hit with "Son of a Preacher Man," but her career trailed off into a slurry of drug and alcohol abuse. By the mid-1970s she was a session singer in Los Angeles. Repeated comebacks failed until she teamed up with the Pet Shop Boys in 1987 on "What Have I Done to Deserve This?" and the soundtrack for *Scandal* (1988), a film set in the pre-Swinging London of her earliest success. By the 1990s she was a camp icon. Resettling in England, she

battled cancer and in 1998 received the Order of the British Empire. She was posthumously inducted into the Rock and Roll Hall of Fame in 1999.

ERIC CLAPTON

Eric Clapton (born Eric Patrick Clapp, March 30, 1945, Ripley, Surrey, England) was raised by his grandparents after his mother abandoned him at an early age. He began playing the guitar in his teens and briefly studied at the Kingston College of Art. After playing lead guitar with two minor bands, in 1963 he joined the Yardbirds, a rhythm-and-blues group in which his blues-influenced playing and commanding technique began to attract attention. Clapton left the Yardbirds in 1965 when they pursued commercial success with a pop-oriented style. That same year he joined John Mayall's Bluesbreakers, and his guitar playing soon became the group's principal drawing card as it attracted a fanatic following on the London club scene.

In 1966 Clapton left the Bluesbreakers to form a new band with two other virtuoso rock musicians, bassist Jack Bruce and drummer Ginger Baker. This group, Cream, achieved international popularity with its sophisticated, high-volume fusion of rock and blues that featured improvisatory solos. Clapton's mastery of blues form and phrasing, his

Eric Clapton performing. His legendary guitar-playing attracted large crowds to both his solo and group performances. Jeremy Fletcher/ Redferns/Getty Images

rapid runs, and his plaintive vibrato were widely imitated by other rock guitarists. The high energy and emotional intensity of his playing on such songs as "Crossroads" and "White Room" set the standard for the rock guitar solo. Cream disbanded in late 1968, however, after having recorded such albums as *Disraeli Gears* (1967), *Wheels of Fire* (1968), and *Goodbye* (1969).

In 1969 Clapton and Baker formed the group Blind Faith with keyboardist-vocalist Steve Winwood and bassist Rick Grech, but the group broke up after recording only one album. Clapton emerged as a capable vocalist on his first solo album, which was released in 1970. He soon assembled a trio of strong session musicians (bassist Carl Radle, drummer Jim Gordon, and keyboardist Bobby Whitlock) into a new band called Derek and the Dominos, with Clapton as lead guitarist, vocalist, and songwriter. The guitarist Duane Allman joined the group in making the classic double album *Layla and Other Assorted Love Songs* (1970), which is regarded as Clapton's masterpiece and a landmark among rock recordings. Disappointed by *Layla*'s lacklustre sales and addicted to heroin, Clapton went into seclusion for two years. Overcoming his addiction, he made a successful comeback with the album *461 Ocean Boulevard* (1974), which included his

hit remake of Bob Marley's "I Shot the Sheriff." On the album Clapton adopted a more relaxed approach that emphasized his songwriting and vocal abilities rather than his guitar playing.

Over the next 20 years Clapton produced a string of albums, including *Slowhand* (1977), *Backless* (1978), *Money and Cigarettes* (1983), *August* (1986), *Unplugged* (1992)—which featured the Top Five hit "Tears in Heaven," written after the death of his son—and *From the Cradle* (1994). He explored his musical influences with a pair of Grammy-winning collaborations: *Riding with the King* (2000) with blues legend B.B. King and *The Road to Escondido* (2006) with roots guitarist J.J. Cale. The critical and commercial success of these albums solidified his stature as one of the world's greatest rock musicians. Clapton was inducted into the Rock and Roll Hall of Fame in 2000.

ROD STEWART AND THE FACES

Although best known as a solo artist, raspy-voiced singer and songwriter, Rod Stewart (born January 10, 1945, London, England) achieved his first exposure and success as a member of several popular groups. After taking an early interest in folk music and rhythm and blues, he was a member of two relatively obscure

London-based bands (Steampacket and Shotgun Express) in the mid-1960s before teaming with the influential guitarist Jeff Beck and future Rolling Stone Ron Wood in the Jeff Beck Group. Stewart's collaboration with Beck ended in 1969 when, after two albums, he was persuaded by guitarist Wood (who had been fired by Beck) to join the Faces.

Formerly the Small Faces, the band—also comprising bassist Ronnie Lane (born April 1, 1946, London), keyboard player Ian McLagan (born May 12, 1945, Houslow), and Kenny Jones (born September 16, 1948, London)—played bluesy rock that appealed to Stewart's long-standing interest in rhythm and blues. During the early 1970s the raucous Faces were among Britain's most popular live performers, and their album *A Nod's as Good as a Wink...to a Blind Horse* (1971) remains highly regarded. Nonetheless, Stewart, determined not to be constrained by the group format, pursued a parallel solo career during his tenure with the Faces (1969–75).

Released in 1969, his first solo album, *An Old Raincoat Won't Ever Let You Down* (also released as *The Rod Stewart Album*), was commercially disappointing, but its mixture of original and cover songs would prove to be a successful formula for Stewart. *Gasoline Alley* (1970) sold better and was well received by critics, but it hardly suggested what would happen in 1971. *Every Picture Tells a Story* became the first record to top the charts in Britain and the United States simultaneously, the single "Maggie Mae" repeated the feat, and *Rolling Stone* magazine named Stewart "rock star of the year." His next album, *Never a Dull Moment* (1972), and its single "You Wear It Well" were also hits, as Stewart's solo work eclipsed his efforts with the Faces. Among other subsequent hits, including Stewart's version of Cat Stevens's "The First Cut Is the Deepest," was "Tonight's the Night," the largest-selling single of 1976; however, the critical success that Stewart had enjoyed was fast approaching an end. The hits continued to come (including the chart-topping "Do Ya Think I'm Sexy" in the late 1970s and a number of Top Ten hits in the 1980s), but increasingly Stewart wrote and recorded fewer of his own songs. His version of the 1985 Tom Waits song "Downtown Train" (1989) was the high point of a later career dominated by covers. Stewart was inducted into the Rock and Roll Hall of Fame in 1994, and he was made a Commander of the British Empire in 2007.

CHAPTER 5

Woody and His Fellow Travelers

The peculiarity of Britain's beat boom—in which would-be pop stars such as the Beatles turned arty while would-be blues musicians such as the Rolling Stones turned pop—had a dramatic effect in the United States, not only on consumers but also on musicians, on the generation who had grown up on rock and roll but grown out of it and into more serious sounds, such as urban folk. The Beatles' success suggested that it was possible to enjoy the commercial, mass-cultural power of rock and roll while remaining an artist. The immediate consequence was folk rock. Folk musicians, led by Bob Dylan, went electric, amplified their instruments, and sharpened their beat. Dylan in particular showed that a pop song could be both a means of social commentary (protest) and a form of self-expression (poetry).

FOLK AS SUCH

Folk music—that music created anonymously by the American underclass—was as old as the country itself, but the *concept* of folk music was of more recent vintage. After the Civil War academic folklorists began collecting traditional songs, including spirituals, Appalachian mountain music, and English and Celtic ballads. The standard English-language folk ballad, the traditional folk ballad, is also sometimes called the Child ballad in deference to Francis Child, a professor at Harvard University who compiled the definitive English collection in the mid-19th century. Child accumulated in the Harvard library one of the largest folklore collections in existence, studied manuscript rather than printed versions of old ballads, and investigated songs and stories in other languages that were related to the English and Scottish ballads.

Folklorists were not alone in pursuing this music, however. By the 1920s the American recording industry had begun to take off, and the search for new products by early record labels such as Victor and OKeh took them to the South, where they found a wellspring of traditional music and musicians. In rural communities in Virginia, North Carolina, Tennessee, and elsewhere they found and recorded fiddlers such as "Fiddlin'" John Carson and banjo players such as "millbilly" Charlie Poole and Uncle Dave Macon. Others, such Virginia singer-guitarist Pop Stoneham, and Dock Boggs, a guitarist, singer, and songwriter who was much influenced by the blues, made the journey to New York City to offer up their talents. In the early 1930s, the Carter Family, whose "mountain" harmonies became staples of both country and folk music, and Jimmie Rodgers, the "Singing Brakeman"—whose version of country music, like that of Boggs, was deeply indebted to the blues— became even bigger recording stars, though as country music moved in a more commercial direction their lasting influence would be as much on later folk musicians as it would be on country and western performers.

Folklorist John Lomax and his son Alan, working with field recording equipment supplied by the Library of Congress, visited prisons during their swing through the South, believing that they would find traditional African American music among the isolated population of prisoners. Their biggest "discovery," a convict named Huddie Ledbetter but better known as Leadbelly, would become one of the most important influences on the development of American folk music. In 1934, after his early release, Leadbelly went on tour, initially under the guidance of John Lomax, and made a series of landmark recordings. As blues became electrified after World War II, the lasting influence of the acoustic blues of Leadbelly would be more on folk musicians than on rhythm and blues.

The onset of the Great Depression, however, would dramatically curtail recording and stall the careers of many of the performers already mentioned, as Americans had little money for the pursuit of leisure. Yet, it was during the Depression that arguably the country's most important and influential folksinger and songwriter, Woody Guthrie, entered upon the scene. An Oklahoman who took to the road at the height of the Dust Bowl era, he frequented hobo and migrant camps on his way to California, where he first popularized his songs about the plight of Dust Bowl refugees, en route to becoming a mythic figure.

WOODY GUTHRIE

Woody Guthrie (born Woodrow Wilson Guthrie, July 14, 1912, Okemah, Oklahoma, U.S.—died October 3, 1967, New York, New York), the third of five children, was the son of a onetime cowboy, land speculator, and local Democratic politician who named him after Pres. Woodrow Wilson. His mother, who introduced her children to a wide variety of music, was thought to be mentally ill and was institutionalized when Guthrie was a teenager. Her erratic behaviour was actually caused by Huntington's disease, a hereditary neurological disorder about which little was known at the time and which would later afflict Guthrie, too. The family lived near the relocated Creek nation in Okemah, Oklahoma, a small agricultural and railroad town that boomed

in the 1920s when oil was discovered in the area. The effect on the town and its people of the decline that followed the boom sensitized the young Guthrie to others' suffering, which he had also experienced firsthand through the calamities that befell his splintering family. (Guthrie paid particular attention to this period of his life in his autobiographical novel *Bound for Glory* [1943].)

BOUND FOR GLORY

Soon after his mother's institutionalization, Guthrie began "rambling" for the first time, coming to love life on the road. Though he often left Okemah to travel during his teens, he always returned to continue his high school education. At age 19 he relocated to Pampa, Texas, where he married Mary Jennings, with whom he had three children. When the Great Depression deepened and drought turned a large section of the Great Plains into the Dust Bowl, making it impossible for Guthrie to support his family, he again took to the road. Like so many other displaced people from the region (collectively called "Okies" regardless of whether they were Oklahomans), he headed for California, playing his guitar and harmonica and singing in taverns, taking odd jobs, and visiting hobo camps as he traveled by freight train, hitchhiked, or simply

Portrait of Woody Guthrie. Frank Driggs Collection/Archive Photos/Getty Images

walked westward. In Los Angeles in 1937, he landed a spot performing on the radio, first with his cousin, Jack Guthrie, then with Maxine Crissman, who called herself Lefty Lou. At that time Guthrie began songwriting in earnest, giving voice to the struggles of the dispossessed and downtrodden while celebrating their indominitable spirit in songs such as "Do Re Mi," "Pretty Boy Floyd," and "Dust Bowl Refugee."

THE MINSTREL OF MERMAID AVENUE

Guthrie's politics became increasingly leftist, and by the time he moved to New York City in 1940 he had become an important musical spokesman for labour and populist sentiments, embraced by left-leaning intellectuals and courted by communists. In New York, to which he had brought his family, Guthrie became one of the principal songwriters for the Almanac Singers, a group of activist performers—including Leadbelly, Pete Seeger, and Cisco Houston—who used their music to attack fascism and support humanitarian and leftist causes.

In 1941 Guthrie made his first recordings, with folklorist Alan Lomax, and traveled to the Pacific Northwest, where a commission to write songs in support of federal dam building and electrification projects produced such well-known compositions as "Grand Coulee Dam" and "Roll On Columbia." Back in New York after serving as a merchant marine during World War II, his first marriage having ended in divorce, Guthrie married Marjorie (Greenblatt) Mazia, a Martha Graham Dance Company dancer with whom he would have four children (including son Arlo, who would become an important singer-songwriter in his own right in the 1960s).

PILGRIMAGE TO GREYSTONE HOSPITAL

As the political tide in the United States turned conservative and then reactionary during the 1950s, Guthrie and his folksinger friends in New York kept alive the flame of activist music making. He continued writing and performing politically charged songs that inspired the American folk revival of the 1960s. At the head of the revival were performers such as Bob Dylan, Joan Baez, and Phil Ochs, who came to pay homage to Guthrie in his hospital room in New Jersey, to which he was confined beginning in 1954, after his increasingly erratic actions were finally and correctly diagnosed as the result of Huntington's disease. Among the more than 1,000 songs that Guthrie wrote were a number of remarkable children's songs written in the language and from the perspective of childhood, as well as some of the most lasting and influential songs in the canon of American music, not least "So Long, It's Been Good to Know Yuh" (legal title: "So Long It's Been Good to Know You", also known as "Dusty Old Dust"), "Hard Traveling," "Blowing Down This Old Dusty Road," "Union Maid," and (inspired by John Steinbeck's *The Grapes of Wrath*) "Tom Joad." Probably the most famous of his works is "This Land Is Your Land," which became a pillar of the civil rights movement of the 1960s.

At the time of his death in 1967, Guthrie had already begun to assume legendary stature as a folk figure, and his influence on such pivotal singer-songwriters as Bob Dylan and Bruce Springsteen was immense. A film version of his book *Bound for Glory* appeared in 1976, and in 1998 Billy Bragg and alternative rockers Wilco released the critically acclaimed *Mermaid Avenue*, a collection of previously unrecorded lyrics by Guthrie that they had set to music; *Mermaid Avenue Vol. II* followed in 2000.

THE ALMANAC AND HEADLINE SINGERS

On the eve of World War II, New York City had become the locus of American folk music, largely because of the presence of Guthrie and the Almanac Singers, whose influence far outlived the short tenure of the group. Founded by Pete Seeger, Lee Hays, and Millard Lampell, the Almanac Singers lived communally in a house (known as the Almanac House) where they conducted "hootenanny" singalongs and rent parties, sang for children, and rewrote traditional songs to fit a leftist, pro-union political agenda that for a significant period of time was in line with that of the Communist Party. Perhaps the most important member of the group was Guthrie, though enumerating the full lineup of the Almanacs is complicated by their philosophical commitment to personal anonymity for the group's members. Leadbelly and bluesmen Sonny Terry and Brownie McGhee were guests at Almanac House and performed with the group. Leadbelly, McGhee, Terry, Josh White, and others also performed with Guthrie as the Headline Singers. The Almanacs' early party-line opposition to involvement in World War II ultimately undermined their acceptance by many Americans even after the group stridently supported the war effort after the advent of the pact between Nazi Germany and the Soviet Union in 1939.

LEADBELLY

Musical from childhood, Leadbelly (born Huddie William Ledbetter,

Leadbelly performing at a school in New York City. Encyclopædia Britannica, Inc.

January 21, 1885?, Jeter Plantation, near Mooringsport, La., U.S.—died December 6, 1949, New York, New York) played accordion, 6- and 12-string guitar, bass, and harmonica. He led a wandering life, learning songs by absorbing oral tradition. For a time he worked as an itinerant musician with Blind Lemon Jefferson. In 1918 he was imprisoned in Texas for murder. According to tradition he won his early release in 1925 by singing a song for the governor of Texas when he visited the prison.

Resuming a life of drifting, Leadbelly was imprisoned for attempted murder in 1930 in the Angola, La., prison farm. There he was "discovered" by the folklorists John Lomax and Alan Lomax. A campaign spearheaded by the Lomaxes secured his release in 1934, and he embarked on a concert tour of eastern colleges. Subsequently he published 48 songs and commentary (1936) about Depression-era conditions of blacks and recorded extensively. His first commercial recordings were made for the American Record Corporation, which did not take advantage of his huge folk repertory but rather encouraged him to sing blues. He settled in New York City in 1937. He struggled to make enough money, and in 1939–40 he was jailed again, this time for assault. When he was released, he worked with Woody Guthrie, Sonny Terry, Brownie McGhee, and others

as the Headline Singers, performed on radio, and, in 1945, appeared in a short film. In 1949, shortly before his death, he gave a concert in Paris.

Leadbelly died penniless, but within six months his song "Goodnight, Irene" had become a million-record hit for the singing group the Weavers; along with other pieces from his repertoire, among them "The Midnight Special" and "Rock Island Line," it became a standard.

Leadbelly's legacy is extraordinary. His recordings reveal his mastery of a great variety of song styles and his prodigious memory; his repertory included more than 500 songs. His rhythmic guitar playing and unique vocal accentuations make his body of work both instructive and compelling. His influence on later musicians—including Eric Clapton, Bob Dylan, Janis Joplin, and Kurt Cobain—was immense.

BROWNIE MCGHEE

The son of a singer and guitarist, Brownie McGhee (born Walter Brown McGhee, November 30, 1915, Knoxville, Tennessee, U.S—died February 16, 1996, Oakland, California) developed an interest in the guitar at about age six and was taught by his sister to play the piano at age eight. He was impressed by itinerant blues musicians and dropped out of high school in the late

3 1613 00450 5650

CALUMET CITY PUBLIC LIBRARY

ALAN LOMAX

After studying at Harvard University, the University of Texas at Austin (B.A., 1936), and Columbia University, Alan Lomax (born January 15, 1915, Austin, Texas, U.S.—died July 19, 2002, Sarasota, Florida) toured the prisons of the American Deep South with his father, John Lomax, recording folk-song performances for the Archive of American Song of the Library of Congress. During this tour they discovered the great blues singer Leadbelly. Lomax was responsible for introducing to American audiences other folk and blues artists, including Woody Guthrie, Muddy Waters, Josh White, and Burl Ives. In 1938 he made a series of recordings with the jazz pianist Jelly Roll Morton. From 1951 to 1958 he was in Europe, recording hundreds of folk songs in Great Britain, Italy, and Spain.

Alan Lomax performing at the Mountain Music Festival, Asheville, N.C. Library of Congress, Washington, D.C. (Digital File Number: LC-DIG-ppmsc-00433)

A profound folklorist who was also interested in the historical and social origins of jazz, Lomax wrote an outstanding biography of Jelly Roll Morton, *Mr. Jelly Roll* (1950). *The Folk Songs of North America in the English Language* was published in 1960. His work in cantometrics (the statistical analysis of singing styles correlated with anthropological data), which he developed with Victor Grauer, is the most comprehensive study of folk song as yet undertaken. *Cantometrics: A Handbook and Training Method* appeared in 1976. Lomax also wrote and directed the documentary *The Land Where the Blues Began* (1985). In 1997 the Alan Lomax Collection debuted on Rounder Records. The series featured more than 100 albums of music recorded by Lomax.

1920s to perform for carnivals, minstrel shows, dances, and informal gatherings throughout Tennessee. In the mid-1930s he led his own washboard band. McGhee first met Sonny Terry in North Carolina in 1939 and worked with him and the singer Paul Robeson in Washington, D.C., in 1940. Settling in New York City in the early 1940s, he roomed with Terry and the blues musician Leadbelly while the three performed in the Headline Singers. Terry and McGhee's partnership began in 1941 and lasted (with frequent interruptions) until the late 1970s. From 1942 to 1950 McGhee ran his own music school, Home of the Blues, in Harlem.

McGhee's first recordings were for the OKeh label in 1940; he later recorded extensively with Terry and others, exhibiting an authentic rural style. He appeared in Tennessee Williams's play *Cat on a Hot Tin Roof* on Broadway (1955–57) and toured with that show. McGhee recorded several motion-picture soundtracks, including for *A Face in the Crowd* (1957).

SONNY TERRY

Blinded in childhood accidents, Sonny Terry (born Saunders Terrell, October 24, 1911, Greensboro, Georgia, U.S.—died March 11, 1986, Mineola, New York) was raised by musical parents and developed a harmonica style that imitated sounds ranging from moving trains to barnyard animals, often using his voice while playing these effects. He was influenced by the harmonica player DeFord Bailey, who broadcast nationally on the radio program Grand Ole Opry. Terry traveled as an itinerant musician from 1929 through the 1930s, working with Blind Boy Fuller and recording with him in 1937–40.

After meeting McGhee in 1939 and performing with him and Robeson, Terry recorded with his soon-to-be longtime partner for the first time in 1941. Subsequently they recorded extensively and toured internationally, becoming a popular nightclub, concert, and folk, blues, and heritage festival attraction. During his long career, Terry also performed with such bluesmen as Blind Gary Davis, Mississippi John Hurt, and Big Bill Broonzy. Terry appeared in the Broadway musical *Finian's Rainbow* (1947–48) and the play *Cat on a Hot Tin Roof* (1955–57).

WASN'T THAT A TIME?: NEW YORK CITY FOLK IN THE 1940S AND '50S

After the war, New York City remained at the centre of American folk music. Seeger, Guthrie, and others formed People's Songs, dedicated to spreading political music both through performance and the publication of agitprop songs in a magazine of the same name that would after a short period evolve into folk music's most lasting voice, the magazine *Sing Out!*. Much as *Sing Out!* had grown out of People's Songs, so, too, did the period's most important folk group, the Weavers, evolve from the roots of the Almanac Singers.

THE WEAVERS

In 1948 ex-Almanacs Seeger and Lee Hays (born 1914, Little Rock, Arkansas, U.S.—died August 26, 1981, Croton-on-Hudson, New York) recruited Ronnie Gilbert (born c. 1927, New York, New York) and guitarist Fred Hellerman (born May 13, 1927, New York) to form the Weavers. They built up an extensive repertoire of traditional folk ballads and new songs, making their mark at the Village Vanguard in New York City's Greenwich Village in 1949. The quartet gained almost instant commercial success on college campuses, in concert, and on several records. Amid accusations of communist sympathies during the Red Scare, however, they were blacklisted. Finding it increasingly difficult to make concert bookings or to sell records, the group disbanded between 1952 and 1955, when Seeger and Hays were called before the House Committee on Un-American Activities.

THE RED SCARE

One of the issues of the 1952 U.S. national election was the fear of the spread of communism. Maoists had taken over mainland China in 1949, the same year the Soviets detonated their first atomic bomb, and in 1950 former U.S. State Department official Alger Hiss was convicted of perjury for having denied being a Russian agent when questioned by the House Committee on Un-American Activities. This committee, first established in 1938, was resurrected during this period to investigate people suspected of posing a threat to national security, and spectacular public hearings were held that added to the general state of paranoia. The entertainment industry was especially vulnerable to investigative efforts because the exposure of well-known persons was of great interest to the press and because many feared that the large audiences commanded by entertainers might make the consequences of their political intentions all the more insidious.

The paranoia fostered by the anticommunist movement became known as the "Red Scare." It affected television differently from the way it had affected the movie industry. Because TV was financed by advertising dollars, anticommunist groups could get quick results by threatening to organize boycotts of the goods produced by the sponsor of a show that employed a "blacklisted" individual, whether a performer or a member of the production staff. Afraid of having their products associated with anything "un-American," sponsors would often respond by either firing the suspect from the show they were producing or, if they were sponsoring a show produced by the network, asking the network to do so.

In June 1950 the publishers of *Counterattack: The Newsletter of Facts on Communism* issued a compact user-friendly guide that listed 151 entertainment industry employees whom they suspected of communist activities. The pamphlet, *Red Channels: The Report of Communist Influence in Radio and Television,* included many well-known writers (Dashiell Hammett, Dorothy Parker, Arthur Miller), directors (Elia Kazan, Edward Dmytryk, Orson Welles), actors (Edward G. Robinson, Burgess Meredith, Ruth Gordon), composers (Leonard Bernstein, Aaron Copland), and singers (Lena Horne, Pete Seeger). Decision makers at advertising agencies and networks read the report, which caused the casts and staff of several shows to be changed and which destroyed several careers.

Sen. Joseph R. McCarthy, a Republican from Wisconsin, made anticommunism his issue and became the "star" of the anticommunist frenzy. He made spectacular accusations in public, claiming at one point that a spy ring of "card-carrying communists" was operating in the State Department with the full knowledge of the secretary of state. McCarthyism became a watchword of the times, referring to the blacklisting, guilt-by-inference, and harassment tactics that the senator used. Although McCarthy used the media to disseminate his beliefs, it was also the media that accelerated his downfall.

In 1954 broadcast journalist Edward R. Murrow produced a notable television exposé of the dubious tactics used by McCarthy. Although public opinion about McCarthy did not completely change overnight, the broadcast was the beginning of the end for the senator. The following month, on April 22, hearings began regarding McCarthy's accusations of subversive activity in the army. McCarthy's charges, which were mostly fabricated, did not hold up to close scrutiny, and the Senate voted to condemn his actions.

The Weavers reunited when a one-off Christmas concert at Carnegie Hall sparked new interest in their music and message. After Seeger quit in 1958 to pursue a solo career, he was replaced by Erik Darling (born September 25, 1933, Baltimore, Maryland—died August 3, 2008, Chapel Hill, North Carolina) from 1958 to 1962, Frank Hamilton (born October 3, 1934, New York) in 1962–63, and Bernie Krause (born

December 8, 1938, Detroit, Michigan) in 1963.

The Weavers, who officially disbanded in 1963, made numerous songs into modern classics, including the Israeli folk song "Tzena, Tzena, Tzena," "Good Night Irene" (by Leadbelly), "So Long, It's Been Good to Know Yuh" (Guthrie), "Kisses Sweeter Than Wine" (Hellerman), and such Seeger-Hays compositions as "If I Had a Hammer" and "Lonesome Traveler." An acclaimed documentary film, *Wasn't That a Time*, chronicled

Pete Seeger performing. George Pickow/Michael Ochs Archives/Getty Images

their 1980 reunion concert in New York City's Carnegie Hall.

PETE SEEGER

Having been at the centre of both the Almanac Singers and the Weavers, Pete Seeger (born May 3, 1919, New York, New York) holds a special place in the history of American folk music. At the head of his musically gifted family were his father, the influential musicologist Charles Seeger, and his mother, Constance, a violin instructor at Juilliard. But it was perhaps the introspective poems of his uncle, Alan Seeger, that most inspired Pete's songwriting. Leaving Harvard after two years in 1938, Seeger hitchhiked and rode freight trains around the country, gathering country ballads, work songs, and hymns and developing a remarkable virtuosity on the five-string banjo. With the Almanacs he appeared at union halls, farm meetings, and wherever his populist political sentiments were welcome. These left-wing political associations would haunt him later as a member of the Weavers, when the group was blacklisted by much of the entertainment industry. After leaving the Weavers in 1958, Seeger usually worked alone or with his family (brother Mike was a member of New Lost City Ramblers; sister Peggy, a singer and multi-instrumentalist,

became one of the driving forces behind the British folk music revival with Ewan McColl, her partner in life and in music making). As a solo performer, he was still a victim of blacklisting, especially after his 1961 conviction for contempt of Congress stemming from his refusal in 1955 to answer questions posed to him by the House Committee on Un-American Activities concerning his political activities. Although Seeger's conviction was overturned the following year in an appeal, for several years afterward the major networks refused to allow him to make television appearances. In later years the controversy surrounding the performer gradually subsided.

A beloved fixture at folk festivals, Seeger was given major credit for fostering the growth of the hootenanny (a gathering of performers playing and singing for each other, often with audience participation) as a characteristically informal and personal style of entertainment. Among the many songs that he wrote himself or in collaboration with others were "Where Have All the Flowers Gone?," "If I Had a Hammer," "Kisses Sweeter Than Wine," and "Turn, Turn, Turn." His *The Incompleat Folksinger* (1972) is a collection of his writings on the history of folk songs, civil rights, and performers in his lifetime.

In the 1970s and '80s he was active in a program to remove pollution from the Hudson River, building the Hudson River sloop *Clearwater*, promoting festivals for its maintenance, and engaging in environmental demonstrations, particularly antinuclear ones. During this period Seeger also performed regularly with singer-songwriter Arlo Guthrie, Woody Guthrie's son.

By the 1990s Seeger had transcended the accusations of the McCarthy era, and he was regarded as a cherished American institution. The motto inscribed on his banjo—"This machine surrounds hate and forces it to surrender"—seemed to have been proven correct. In 1994 he was awarded a National Medal of Arts, the first of many honours that he received as the century approached its turn. Seeger was inducted into the Rock and Roll Hall of Fame in 1996, and the following year he received his first Grammy Award, for *Pete* (1996). In 2009 he won a second Grammy, for *At 89* (2008), a collection that found the artist approaching his 90th birthday with undiminished spirit and hope. In 2010 he released *Tomorrow's Children*, an album dedicated to environmental awareness that Seeger recorded with the Rivertown Kids, a group of students who attended middle school near Seeger's home. The album won a Grammy for best musical album for children in 2011. Seeger's "musical autobiography" *Where Have All the Flowers Gone* was published in 1996.

BURL IVES

Another singer who was very much a fixture of the New York City folk scene in the 1950s was Burl Ives (born Charles Icle Ivanhoe Ives, June 14, 1909, Jasper county, Illinois, U.S.—died April 14, 1995, Anacortes, Washington), who began performing at age four and learned Scottish, English, and Irish ballads from his grandmother. He left college to hitchhike around the U.S., collecting songs from hoboes and drifters. Soon after his postwar concert debut in New York City, he was hailed by Carl Sandburg as "the mightiest ballad singer of this or any other century." He recorded more than 100 albums and had hits with "I Know an Old Lady (Who Swallowed a Fly)," "The Blue Tail Fly," "Big Rock Candy Mountain," "Frosty the Snowman," and "A Little Bitty Tear." He also was an actor and appeared in many films—including *East of Eden* (1955), *Desire Under the Elms* (1958), *Cat on a Hot Tin Roof* (1958), and won an Academy Award as best supporting actor for his performance in *The Big Country* (1958).

CHAPTER 6

Woody's Children: The Folk Revival

Folk music, especially political folk music, may have been driven underground by the McCarthy era, but it persisted throughout the 1950s in Greenwich Village. Beginning in the early 20th century and especially since the Beat movement of the early 1950s, the Village had been a mecca for creative radicals—artists, poets, jazz musicians—from all over the United States. The Village Vanguard remained an important venue for folk in the 1950s, but it was from Washington Square Park in the Village that the huge resurgence that became known as the folk revival emanated. There, on Sundays, an ever-increasing crowd of folkies gathered with their guitars to play, sing, listen, and trade songs. The Beats were still on the scene, and some of those who ventured to the Village on weekends to engage in bohemian life or to observe "beatniks" came upon the scene in Washington Square. Word spread.

Equally important to the folk revival was the runaway success of the Kingston Trio's "Tom Dooley," a polished remake of a traditional death ballad that became a huge national hit and sent waves of young people to music stores in search of acoustic guitars. In the process, in the early 1960s, scores of collegiate-looking folk groups in the image of the Trio sprung up, among them the Brothers Four, the Limelighters, and the Chad Mitchell Trio. Their songs, though usually traditional in nature, were generally apolitical. Their version of folk music was popular and distinctly commercial. A television program, *Hootenanny*, came into being in 1963 to showcase this music with weekly stops at a different college campus. Cambridge, Massachusetts, and Berkeley, California, became new centres of folk music making and performance.

A new generation of "purist" folkies, most of them more concerned with authenticity than commercial success, also began to arrive in Greenwich Village from all over the country. For many of them a huge source of inspiration was the *Anthology of American Folk Music*, a collection of popular recordings from the 1920s and '30s assembled by eccentric anthropologist and experimental filmmaker Harry Smith and released on Folkways records in 1952. The anthology included the likes of Dock Boggs, the Carter Family, Uncle Dave Macon, and Charlie Poole, among dozens of others that critic Greil Marcus would later characterize as musical denizens of the "old, weird America." In coffeehouses such as the Cafe Wha? on McDougal Street and Gerde's Folk City at 11 West 4th Street, Fred Neil, Bob Dylan, Phil Ochs, and Paul Simon played for a few dollars to small crowds, discovering which songs worked and what to say between them. There was little obvious connection between this scene and the folk music that was appearing on the pop charts until 1963, when two of Dylan's songs became Top Ten hits for Peter, Paul and Mary (Albert Grossman was the manager of both acts).

THE KINGSTON TRIO

In San Francisco in 1957 Dave Guard (born October 19, 1934, San Francisco, California, U.S.—died March 22, 1991, Rollinsford, New Hampshire), Bob Shane (born February 1, 1934, Hilo, Hawaii), and Nick Reynolds (born July 27, 1933, San Diego, California—died October 1, 2008) founded the Kingston Trio, the group that helped spark the folk music revival of the 1960s. With a repertoire that drew on traditional folk material but eschewed the left-wing sympathies typical of many American folk performers in the first half of the 20th century, the Trio conveyed the lighthearted optimism of mainstream Americans at the onset of the 1960s. With their tight harmonies and clean-cut image, the Trio scored a breakthrough hit with "Tom Dooley" (1958), which earned them their first Grammy Award for best country and western performance (folk music was not a category). That song was followed by such hit singles as "M.T.A.," "A Worried Man," and "The Wanderer" and a series of chart-topping albums—including

ELEKTRA RECORDS: VILLAGE FOLK TO "RIDERS ON THE STORM"

Formed in 1950 by Jac Holzman, who initially ran it from his dormitory at St. John's College, in Annapolis, Maryland, Elektra became one of the top folk labels alongside Vanguard, Folkways, and Prestige. Simply recorded albums by Jean Ritchie, Josh White, and Theodore Bikel achieved substantial sales without the need for expensive marketing or hit singles, even after Elektra moved to offices on West 14th Street near Greenwich Village. But, while the other labels mostly stuck to traditional notions of folk, Elektra adapted in response to the emergence of folk rock, recording Judy Collins, Tom Rush, and Phil Ochs. By the end of the 1960s it had merged with Warner and Atlantic to form one of the major companies in the recording industry.

Inspired by British reinterpretations of Elektra's folk repertoire (particularly the Animals' 1964 version of "House of the Rising Sun," previously associated with Josh White), artists-and-repertoire man Paul Rothchild encouraged amplified versions of folk and blues. He pulled together the work of various artists in the *Blues Project* concept album (1964) and signed the Chicago-based Paul Butterfield Blues Band, featuring guitar prodigy Mike Bloomfield. Most prescient of all, he discovered and produced the band that was to become one of the most successful and influential West Coast acts of the era, the Los Angeles-based Doors.

Kingston Trio at Large (1959; which won a Grammy), *Here We Go Again* (1959), and *String Along* (1960); 13 of the trio's albums reached the Top 10. In 1961 Guard left the group and was replaced by singer-songwriter John Stewart (born September 5, 1939, San Diego). Stewart was playing the guitar and banjo and had written his first song by the age of 10. Before joining the Trio, in 1958 Stewart had formed the Cumberland Three, which had recorded three albums. (He later gained solo fame as the composer of the Monkees' hit "Daydream Believer" and as a singer-songwriter.) Though the Kingston Trio was debunked by "serious" folk musicians, its commercial success paved the way for record-industry and audience acceptance of folk performers such as Joan Baez, Bob Dylan, and Peter, Paul and Mary. As the social and political landscape changed, the Trio's popularity waned; the group disbanded in 1967.

THE CLANCY BROTHERS AND TOMMY MAKEM

Tommy Makem (born Thomas James Makem, November 4, 1932, Keady, County Armagh, Northern Ireland—died August 1, 2007, Dover, New Hampshire, U.S.), the son of traditional Irish vocalist Sarah Makem, immigrated to the U.S. in 1955 to become an actor, but he found greater success as a singer, teaming up with the Irish-born Liam (born September 2, 1935, Carrick-on-Suir, County Tipperary, Ireland—died Dec. 4, 2009, Cork), Tom (born October 29, 1924, Carrick-on-Suir, County Tipperary— died November 7, 1990, Cork), and Paddy (born Patrick Clancy, March 7, 1922, Carrick-on-Suir, County Tipperary, —died November 11, 1998, Carrick-on-Suir) Clancy to form the Clancy Brothers and Tommy Makem. Together they popularized and rejuvenated traditional, often sombre, Celtic music in the U.S. and throughout the world during the 1960s. The quartet released its first two albums in 1959, *The Rising of the Moon: Irish Songs of Rebellion* and *Come Fill Your Glass with Us*, before reaching a wider audience with a television appearance in 1961 on *The Ed Sullivan Show*. Later that year Makem also produced his debut solo album, *The Songs of Tommy Makem*. From 1973 Liam Clancy pursued a solo career and starred in a Canadian TV program. Makem and Clancy later reunited (1975–88) as a duo.

HARRY BELAFONTE

Harry Belafonte (born Harold George Belafonte, Jr., March 1, 1927, New York, New York, U.S.) was the son of immigrants from the Caribbean islands of Martinique and Jamaica, and he lived with his mother during her 1935–40 return to Jamaica. He left high school to serve in the U.S. Navy in the mid-1940s; after returning to New York City he studied drama at Erwin Piscator's Dramatic Workshop, where a singing role led to nightclub engagements and a recording contract as a pop singer. In 1950 he became a folksinger, learning songs at the Library of Congress' American folk-song archives. He sang West Indian folk songs as well, in nightclubs and theatres, and his handsome appearance added to his appeal as a frequent performer on television variety programs. With hit recordings such as "Day-O (Banana Boat Song)" and "Jamaica Farewell," he initiated a fad for calypso music; in the mid-1950s his *Belafonte* and *Mark Twain and Other Folk Favorites* were the first of his series of hit folk-song albums.

Belafonte was the male lead (but did not sing) in the film musical *Carmen Jones* (1954), a success that led to a starring role in the film *Island in the Sun* (1957). He also produced the film *Odds Against Tomorrow* (1959), in which he acted, and in the 1960s became the first African American television producer. He helped introduce South African singer Miriam Makeba and Greek singer Nana Mouskouri to American audiences. A civil-rights activist, he was also active in charitable work. In the 1970s, when his singing career was a secondary occupation, he was featured in the films *Buck and the Preacher* (1972) and *Uptown Saturday Night* (1974).

DAVE VAN RONK

A masterful performer of blues and jazz as well as folk, Dave Van Ronk (born June 30, 1936, Brooklyn, New York, U.S.—died February 10, 2002, New York City) was a longtime fixture on the East Coast music scene. He helped launch the careers of younger musicians such as Bob Dylan, Tom Paxton, and Suzanne Vega. Van Ronk's reputation was based on his interpretation of material by others rather than on his own compositions.

PHIL OCHS

Phil Ochs (born December 19, 1940, El Paso, Texas, U.S.—died April 9, 1976, Far Rockaway, New York) is best remembered for the protest songs he wrote in the 1960s on topics ranging from the Vietnam War to civil rights. While studying journalism at Ohio State University, Ochs became interested in the folk music of Woody Guthrie and Pete Seeger. In 1961 he moved to New York City to pursue songwriting and performing in the hothouse environment of Greenwich Village's folk scene. His first album, *All the News That's Fit to Sing* (1964), reflected his aspirations as a "singing journalist." A wavery tenor, Ochs employed melodic lyricism, strident leftist views, and dry wit to engage listeners. For a time he was seen as the most serious challenger to Bob Dylan as the era's preeminent folksinger. After releasing the successful *Phil Ochs in Concert* album in 1966, he ventured into electric rock and nonpolitical subjects. Ochs played a pivotal role in the founding of the

BROADSIDE

In 1962 Agnes "Sis" Cunningham, a onetime member of the Almanac Singers, and her husband, Gordon Friesen, cofounded the small but inspirational folk-song journal *Broadside*. Although its circulation never topped four figures, the journal proved instrumental in promoting folk music that delivered strong leftist political messages during the 1960s. Among the more than 1,000 songs published in the journal were Bob Dylan's "Blowin' in the Wind" and Pete Seeger's "Waist Deep in the Big Muddy." The journal's name reaches back to one of the earliest products of the printing press, broadsheets, which were about the size of handbills and on which were printed the text of ballads. A crude woodcut often headed the sheet, and under the title it was specified that the ballad was to be sung to the tune of some popular air. Musical notation seldom appeared on the broadsides; those who sold the ballads in the streets and at country fairs sang their wares so that anyone unfamiliar with the tune could learn it by

Detail of an undated broadside ballad distributed in Boston following the execution of Levi Ames for burglary and intended to warn "thoughtless Youth." Library of Congress, Washington, D.C.

listening a few times to the balladmonger's rendition. Before the advent of newspapers, the rhymed accounts of current events provided by the broadside ballads were the chief source of spectacular news. Every sensational public happening was immediately clapped into rhyme and sold on broadsheets.

Youth International Party ("Yippie") and in the demonstrations at the Democratic National Convention in Chicago in 1968. Despite his highly regarded love song "Changes," Ochs never gained the wide popularity he sought. Acutely depressed and creatively spent, he took his own life in 1976.

TOM PAXTON

After studying drama at the University of Oklahoma and serving in the U.S. Army, Tom Paxton (born October 31, 1937, Chicago, Illinois, U.S.) joined the folk music scene in New York City, singing and playing acoustic guitar in small folk clubs. Despite a substantial following as a performer, he became more widely known as a composer. Paxton's work ranged from sorrowful ballads ("The Last Thing on My Mind," "Ramblin' Boy") to topical political and social protest songs ("Whose Garden Was This," "Peace Will Come") to children's tunes ("The Marvelous Toy," "Jennifer's Rabbit"). He was particularly noted for his perceptive lyrics and for his use of insightful humour and satire.

JOAN BAEZ

The daughter of a physicist of Mexican descent whose teaching and research took him to various communities in New York, California, and elsewhere, Joan Baez (born January 9, 1941, Staten Island, New York, U.S) moved often and acquired little formal musical training. Her first instrument was the ukulele, but she soon learned to accompany her clear soprano voice on the guitar. Her first solo album, *Joan Baez*, was released in 1960. Although some considered her voice too pretty, her youthful attractiveness and activist energy put her in the forefront of the 1960s folk music revival, popularizing traditional songs through her performances in coffeehouses, at music festivals, and on television and through her record albums, which were best sellers from 1960 through 1964 and remained popular. She was instrumental in the early career of Bob Dylan, with whom she was romantically involved for several years. (Her relationship with Dylan and with her sister and brother-in-law, the folksinging duo Mimi and Richard Fariña, is chronicled in David Hajdu's *Positively 4th Street* [2001].) Two of the songs with which she is most identified are her 1971 cover of the Band's "The Night They Drove Old Dixie Down" and her own "Diamonds and Rust," which she recorded on her acclaimed album of the same name, issued in 1975.

An active participant in the 1960s protest movement, Baez made free concert appearances for UNESCO, civil rights organizations, and anti-Vietnam War rallies. In 1964 she refused to pay federal taxes that went toward war expenses, and she was jailed twice in 1967. The following year she married David Harris, a leader in the national movement to oppose the draft who served nearly two years in prison for refusing to comply with his draft summons (they divorced in 1973). Baez was in Hanoi in December 1972, delivering Christmas presents and mail to American prisoners of war, when the United States targeted the North Vietnamese capital with the most intense bombing campaign of the war. The title track of her 1973 album "Where Are You Now, My Son?" chronicles the experience; it is a 23-minute spoken-word piece punctuated with sound clips that Baez recorded during the bombing. Throughout the years, she remained deeply committed to social and political causes, lending her voice to many concerts for a variety of causes. Among Baez's other noteworthy recordings are *Very Early Joan* (1982), *Speaking of Dreams* (1989), *Play Me Backwards* (1992), *Gone from Danger* (1997), and *Bowery Songs* (2005). She wrote *Daybreak* (1968), an autobiography, and a memoir titled *And a Voice to Sing With* (1987).

MIMI AND RICHARD FARIÑA

Mimi Fariña (born Margarita Mimi Baez, born April 30, 1945, Stanford, California, U.S.—died July 18, 2001, Mill Valley, California) was the younger sister of Joan Baez and was a well-known performer in her own right. While in Europe she met Richard Fariña (born April 30, 1937?, New York, New York—died April 30, 1966, Carmel, California), who had studied engineering and literature at Cornell University and reputedly had served with the Irish Republican Army in the mid-1950s and later

NEWPORT FOLK FESTIVAL

Founded in Newport, Rhode Island, by music producer George Wein, his business partner Albert Grossman, and several singer-songwriters, the Newport Folk Festival, first staged in 1959, had the aim of showcasing the diversity of American folk music, from rural traditions to urban popular styles. The bill of the inaugural event included Pete Seeger, the newly popular Kingston Trio, and the then unknown singer-songwriter Joan Baez. The event drew an audience of some 13,000 and subsequently became an annual affair, continuing without interruption for more than a decade. Bob Dylan was introduced to the festival crowd in 1963. He proved so popular that he returned in 1964 and again in 1965, when he famously challenged the widely accepted notion that "authentic" folk music was acoustic music. Backed by a blues band using electric amplifiers, his performance was booed by much of the audience. The booing has been interpreted most popularly as an unequivocal commentary on Dylan's "plugged-in" playing, but the actual cause of the commotion has remained controversial.

The Newport Folk Festival began to experience financial difficulties in the late 1960s, and as a result, no production was planned for 1970. Although scheduled to resume in 1971, the festival was ultimately canceled—less than a week before its opening—in the wake of unrest at the Newport Jazz Festival. For the next 15 years, the Newport Folk Festival lay dormant.

Spearheaded by Wein and his company, Festival Productions, Inc., the festival returned in 1985, with some important changes. Whereas the earlier productions had been nonprofit events, the revived version was a for-profit venture. Moreover, evening concerts were discontinued, and the venue was moved away from the Newport downtown area to the nearby Fort Adams State Park, which could accommodate only about 10,000 guests. Although many of the musicians originally slated to perform at the aborted 1971 festival—including Arlo Guthrie and Judy Collins—appeared on the 1985 bill, the festival began to implement a policy of counterbalancing performances by veteran folk musicians with presentations by new artists. In 1986, for instance, the festival gave a spot to the 14-year-old fiddle virtuoso Alison Krauss, who later became a superstar of bluegrass music.

briefly with Fidel Castro's guerrillas in Cuba. A multi-instrumentalist (guitar, dulcimer, and zither) and gifted songwriter, Richard had released an album on which Dylan had performed under the pseudonym "Blind Boy Grunt" before he and Mimi (who primarily played guitar) began performing together. Their highly regarded albums *Celebrations for a Grey Day* (1965) and *Reflections in a Crystal Wind* (1966) were early examples of folk rock, and the duo's performance at the 1965 Newport Folk Festival seemed to promise great things to come.

Richard also wrote fiction. Partially set at Cornell, his first novel, *Been Down So Long It Looks Like Up to Me* (1966; film 1971), was a comic work about the meaning of life, and it provided a portrait of the counterculture on the eve of the 1960s. His novel *Long Time Coming and a Long*

Time Gone was published posthumously in 1969. Autobiographical and episodic, his fiction is humorous and irreverent, with a freewheeling quality reminiscent of the novels of the Beat writers of the 1950s. After Richard's death in a motorcycle accident in 1966, Mimi continued to make recordings, including *Take Heart* (1971), a duo album with Tom Jans. She was also known as the founder of Bread & Roses, a charity that organized musical shows for audiences in nursing homes, hospitals, homeless and drug rehabilitation centres, and correctional facilities.

JUDY COLLINS

A classically trained pianist and self-taught guitarist, Judy Collins (born May 1, 1939, Seattle, Washington, U.S.) performed in folk clubs and coffeehouses from 1959, popularizing works by such songwriters as Bob Dylan, Leonard Cohen, Phil Ochs, Tom Paxton, and Joni Mitchell. She also had great success with cabaret and theatrical songs by Jacques Brel, Kurt Weill, Stephen Sondheim, and Randy Newman. Her biggest hits included Mitchell's "Both Sides Now," Sondheim's "Send in the Clowns," a haunting a cappella version of the spiritual "Amazing Grace," and "Farewell to Tarwathie," a Scottish whaling song accompanied by recordings of humpback whales. Noted for her beauty, especially her startling blue eyes, Collins was reportedly the inspiration for "Suite: Judy Blue Eyes," a hit song by Crosby, Stills and Nash.

LEONARD COHEN

Already established as a poet and novelist (his first book of poems, *Let Us Compare Mythologies*, was published in 1956), Canadian singer-songwriter Leonard Cohen (born September 21, 1934, Montreal, Quebec, Canada) became interested in the Greenwich Village folk scene while living in New York City during the mid-1960s, and he began setting his poems to music. In 1967 Judy Collins recorded two of his songs, "Suzanne" and "Dress Rehearsal Rag," and that same year Cohen began performing in public, including an appearance at Newport. By the end of the year, he had recorded *The Songs of Leonard Cohen*, which included the melancholy "Hey, That's No Way to Say Goodbye." That album was followed by *Songs from a Room* (1969), featuring the now often-covered "Bird on a Wire," and *Songs of Love and Hate* (1971), containing "Famous Blue Raincoat," a ballad in the form of a letter from a cuckold to his wife's lover.

Though some did not care for Cohen's baritone voice and deadpan delivery, he mostly enjoyed critical and commercial success. *Leonard Cohen: Live Songs* (1973) and *New Skin for the Old Ceremony* (1974), which included "Chelsea Hotel No. 2," a frank recollection of a brief sexual encounter with Janis Joplin, further deepened Cohen's standing as a songwriter of exceptional emotional power. His career then took a decided turn for the worse with the disappointing *Death of a Ladies' Man* (1977), a collaboration with legendary producer Phil Spector, whose grandiose style was ill-suited to Cohen's understated songs. For most of the 1980s Cohen was out of favour, but his 1988 album, *I'm Your Man*, included the club hits "First We Take Manhattan" and "Everybody Knows" and introduced his songwriting to a new generation.

After releasing *The Future* (1992), he retired to a Buddhist monastery outside Los Angeles. He emerged in 1999 and returned to the studio,

Leonard Cohen performing. Jan Persson/Redferns/Getty Images

producing *Ten New Songs* (2001) and *Dear Heather* (2004). The critically acclaimed documentary *Leonard Cohen: I'm Your Man* (2005) blended interview and archival footage with performances of Cohen's songs by a variety of musicians.

In 2005 Cohen discovered that his business manager had embezzled some $5 million from his savings, virtually wiping out his retirement fund. While he won a $7.9 million judgment against her the following year, Cohen was unable to recover the money, and

he embarked on a concert tour—his first in 15 years in 2008 to rebuild his finances. One performance from that tour was recorded for the album *Live in London* (2009), a two-disc set which proved that at age 73 Cohen was as vibrant and vital as ever. The aptly titled *Old Ideas* (2012) was a bluesy exploration of familiar Cohen themes—spirituality, love, and loss—that eschewed the synthesized melodies of much of Cohen's post-1980s material in favor of the folk sound of his earliest work. In 2008 he was inducted into the Rock and Roll Hall of Fame, and in 2010 he was honoured with a Grammy Award for lifetime achievement.

PETER, PAUL AND MARY

The connection between the Greenwich Village folk scene and the pop charts was established in 1963, when Peter, Paul and Mary—who shared a manager (Albert Grossman) with Bob Dylan—scored Top Ten Hits with two of Dylan's songs. Peter Yarrow (born May 31, 1938, New York, New York, U.S.), Paul (later Noel Paul) Stookey (born November 30, 1937, Baltimore, Maryland), and Mary Allin Travers (born November 9, 1936, Louisville, Kentucky—died September 16, 2009, Danbury, Connecticut) had met in the Village in 1961 and formed a group. Playing in folk clubs and on college campuses, they built a youthful following with their lyricism, tight harmonies, and spare sound, usually accompanied only by Yarrow and Stookey on acoustic guitars. With their records and television appearances, they popularized both new and traditional folk songs by such songwriters as Woody Guthrie ("This Land Is Your Land"), the Weavers ("If I Had a Hammer"), Bob Dylan ("Blowin' in the Wind"), and Laura Nyro ("And When I Die").

Prominent in the civil rights movement and the struggle against the Vietnam War, Peter, Paul and Mary included protest songs in a repertoire that also featured plaintive ballads and children's songs such as Yarrow's "Puff (the Magic Dragon)," which often is mistakenly interpreted as drug-related. After splitting up in 1970 to pursue solo careers, the trio re-formed to release the album *Reunion* in 1978. In 1986 they celebrated their 25th anniversary with a series of concerts.

ODETTA

African American folk singer Odetta, who was noted especially for her versions of spirituals, became for many the voice of the civil rights movement of the early 1960s. After her father's death in 1937, Odetta (born Odetta Holmes, December 31, 1930, Birmingham, Alabama, U.S.—died December 2, 2008, New York, New York) moved with her mother to Los Angeles. She began classical voice training at age 13, and she earned a degree in classical music from Los Angeles City College. Though she had heard the music of the Deep South as a child, it was not until 1950, on a trip to San Francisco, that she began to appreciate and participate in the emergent folk scene. She soon learned to play the guitar and began to perform traditional songs. Her distinctive blend of folk, blues, ballads, and spirituals was powered by her rich vocal style, wide range, and deep passion. Within a few years her career took off. In the early 1950s she moved to New York City, where she met Pete Seeger and Harry Belafonte, who became loyal supporters. Her debut solo recording, *Odetta Sings Ballads and Blues* (1956), was soon followed by *At the Gate of Horn* (1957). Bob Dylan later said that hearing Odetta on record "turned me on to folk singing." She performed at the Newport Folk Festival four times during 1959–65, and she subsequently appeared on television and in several films.

In the late 1950s and early 1960s, Odetta continued to record as a leading folk musician—although recordings did not do her performances justice. Her music and her politics suited the growing civil rights movement, and in 1963 she sang at the historic March on Washington. Inevitably, as the movement waned and interest in folk music declined, Odetta's following shrank, although she continued to perform. In 1999 Pres. Bill Clinton awarded her the National Medal of Arts, the highest award given in the arts in the United States, and in 2003 she was named a Living Legend by the Library of Congress.

CHAPTER 7

Bob Dylan

Bob Dylan moved from folk to rock music in the 1960s, infusing the lyrics of rock and roll, theretofore concerned mostly with boy-girl romantic innuendo, with the intellectualism of classic literature and poetry. Hailed as the Shakespeare of his generation, Dylan sold more than 58 million albums, wrote more than 500 songs recorded by more than 2,000 artists, performed all over the world, and set the standard for lyric writing.

BOY FROM THE NORTH COUNTRY

Dylan (born Robert Allen Zimmerman, May 24, 1941, Duluth, Minnesota, U.S.) grew up in the northeastern Minnesota mining town of Hibbing, where his father co-owned Zimmerman Furniture and Appliance Co. Taken with the music of Hank Williams, Little Richard, Elvis Presley, and Johnny Ray, he acquired his first guitar in 1955 at age 14 and later, as a high school student, played in a series of rock-and-roll bands. In 1959, just before enrolling at the University of Minnesota in Minneapolis, he served a brief stint playing piano for rising pop star Bobby Vee. While attending college, he discovered the bohemian section of Minneapolis known as Dinkytown. Fascinated by Beat poetry and folksinger Woody Guthrie, he began performing folk music in coffeehouses, adopting the last name Dylan (after the Welsh poet Dylan Thomas).

Restless and determined to meet Guthrie—who was confined to a hospital in New Jersey—he relocated to the East Coast.

TALKIN' NEW YORK

Arriving in late January 1961, Dylan was greeted by a typically merciless New York City winter. A survivor at heart, he relied on the generosity of various benefactors who, charmed by his performances at Gerde's Folk City in Greenwich Village, provided meals and shelter. He quickly built a cult following and within four months was hired to play harmonica for a Harry Belafonte recording session. Responding to Robert Shelton's laudatory *New York Times* review of one of Dylan's live shows in September 1961, talent scout–producer John Hammond investigated and signed him to Columbia Records. There Dylan's unkempt appearance and roots-oriented song material earned him the whispered nickname "Hammond's Folly."

Dylan's eponymous first album was released in March 1962 to mixed reviews. His singing voice—a cowboy lament laced with Midwestern patois, with an obvious nod to Guthrie—confounded many critics. It was a sound that took some getting used to. By comparison, Dylan's second album, *The Freewheelin' Bob Dylan* (released in May 1963), sounded a

clarion call. Young ears everywhere quickly assimilated his quirky voice, which divided parents and children and established him as part of the burgeoning counterculture, "a rebel with a cause." Moreover, his first major composition, "Blowin' in the Wind," served notice that this was no cookie-cutter recording artist. About this time, Dylan signed a seven-year management contract with Albert Grossman, who soon replaced Hammond with another Columbia producer, Tom Wilson.

In April 1963 Dylan played his first major New York City concert, at Town Hall. In May, when he was forbidden to perform "Talkin' John Birch Paranoid Blues" on Ed Sullivan's popular television program, he literally walked out on a golden opportunity. That summer, championed by folk music's doyenne, Joan Baez, Dylan made his first appearance at the Newport Folk Festival and was virtually crowned the king of folk music. The prophetic title song of his next album, *The Times They Are A-Changin'* (1964), provided an instant anthem.

ANOTHER SIDE OF BOB DYLAN

Millions jumped on the bandwagon when the mainstream folk trio Peter, Paul and Mary reached number two on the pop music charts in mid-1963

JOHN HAMMOND

Record producer, promoter, talent scout, and music critic John Hammond (born December 15, 1910, New York, New York, U.S.—died July 10, 1987, New York) discovered and promoted several major figures of popular music, from Count Basie and Billie Holiday in the 1930s to Bob Dylan and Bruce Springsteen during the rock era. A tireless crusader for racial integration in the music business, he is regarded as the most important nonmusician in the history of jazz.

Born into a wealthy New York family, Hammond studied piano and violin as a child and later attended Yale University as a music major. From the age of 10 or 11, he often sneaked away from home or school to visit Harlem, listening to street music, buying records of black artists, or wandering around. He was enormously moved by blues singer Bessie Smith's performance at the Alhambra Theater in 1927; this event was a catalyst in Hammond's lifelong dedication to music promotion, especially the music of black artists. He dropped out of Yale and took a job as a correspondent for *Melody Maker* magazine. In his first successful venture as a record producer, in 1931 he personally funded the recordings of pianist Garland Wilson.

In 1933 Hammond produced a series of recordings with Fletcher Henderson, Benny Carter, and Benny Goodman. In the same year, Hammond produced Bessie Smith's final recording session and Billie Holiday's first. Hammond continued to produce Holiday's sessions through 1937, most of them featuring pianist Teddy Wilson, another Hammond discovery. A lifelong crusader for integration in the music business (and an officer in the NAACP—the National Association for the Advancement of Colored People), Hammond was instrumental in persuading Benny Goodman to accept Wilson and percussionist Lionel Hampton into his small groups and to hire

Fletcher Henderson as his main arranger. In 1936 Hammond heard the Count Basie orchestra on a radio broadcast and subsequently helped bring the band to national prominence. Two years later Hammond organized the first of two historic "Spirituals to Swing" concerts, which chronicled the history of black jazz and blues, at New York City's Carnegie Hall. Hammond's last major discovery of the 1930s was pioneering electric guitarist Charlie Christian, who became a member of Goodman's small groups in 1939.

Hammond worked for several record labels during his career, most importantly with Columbia Records, with which he was associated for many years, on and off. He showed little interest in the bebop movement that emerged after World War II, during which he had served in the military. In the 1950s he produced a highly regarded series of recordings with several swing-era veterans. He was also affiliated with the Newport Jazz Festival (begun in 1954) and wrote articles for newspapers and magazines.

Hammond's enthusiasm returned as he discovered rock music, and he promoted the careers of several great rock musicians—including Bob Dylan, Aretha Franklin, Leonard Cohen, and Bruce Springsteen—during the 1960s and early '70s.

with their version of "Blowin' in the Wind." Dylan was perceived as a singer of protest songs, a politically charged artist with a whole other agenda. (Unlike Elvis Presley, there would be no film of Dylan singing "Rock-a-Hula Baby" surrounded by bikini-clad women.) Dylan spawned imitators at coffeehouses and record labels everywhere. At the 1964 Newport Folk Festival, while previewing songs from *Another Side of Bob Dylan*, he confounded his core audience by performing songs of a personal nature rather than his signature protest repertoire. Although his new lyrics were as challenging as his earlier compositions, a backlash from purist folk fans began and continued for three years as Dylan defied convention at every turn. In December 1963 Dylan befriended Beat poet Allen Ginsberg, and the two would have an important influence on each

Joan Baez (left) and Bob Dylan at the March on Washington, August 28, 1963. Rowland Scherman/NARA

other for years to come. Dylan had already read Beat literature before he left Minnesota, but at this point Ginsberg had a big impact on Dylan's evolving imagery.

On his next album, *Bringing It All Back Home* (1965), electric instruments were openly brandished—a violation of folk dogma—and only two protest songs were included. The folk rock group the Byrds covered "Mr. Tambourine Man" from that album, adding electric 12-string guitar and three-part harmony vocals, and took it to number one on the singles chart. Other rock artists were soon pilfering the Dylan songbook and joining the juggernaut. As Dylan's mainstream audience increased rapidly, his purist folk fans fell off in droves. The maelstrom that engulfed Dylan is captured in *Don't Look Back* (1967), the telling documentary of his 1965 tour of Britain, directed by D.A. Pennebaker.

ALLEN GINSBERG

Allen Ginsberg (born June 3, 1926, Newark, New Jersey, U.S.—died April 5, 1997, New York, New York) grew up in Paterson, New Jersey, where his father, Louis Ginsberg, a poet, taught English. Allen Ginsberg's mother, whom he mourned in his long poem *Kaddish* (1961), was confined for years in a mental hospital. Ginsberg was influenced in his work by the poet William Carlos Williams, particularly toward the use of natural speech rhythms and direct observations of unadorned actuality.

While at Columbia University, where his anarchical proclivities pained the authorities, Ginsberg became close friends with Jack Kerouac and William Burroughs, who were later to be numbered among the Beats. After leaving Columbia in 1948, he traveled widely and worked at a number of jobs from cafeteria floor mopper to market researcher.

Howl, Ginsberg's first published book, laments what he believed to have been the destruction by insanity of the "best minds of [his] generation." Dithyrambic and prophetic, owing something to the romantic bohemianism of Walt Whitman, it also dwells on homosexuality, drug addiction, Buddhism, and Ginsberg's revulsion from what he saw as the materialism and insensitivity of post-World War II America.

Empty Mirror, a collection of earlier poems, appeared along with *Kaddish and Other Poems* in 1961, followed by *Reality Sandwiches* in 1963. *Kaddish*, one of Ginsberg's most important works, is a long confessional poem in which the poet laments his mother's insanity and tries to come to terms with both his relationship to her and with her death. In the early 1960s Ginsberg began a life of ceaseless travel, reading his poetry at campuses and coffee bars, traveling abroad, and engaging in left-wing political activities. He became an influential guru of the American youth counterculture in the late 1960s. He acquired a deeper knowledge of Buddhism, and increasingly a religious element of love for all sentient beings entered his work.

His later volumes of poetry included *Planet News* (1968); *The Fall of America: Poems of These States, 1965–1971* (1972), which won the National Book Award; *Mind Breaths: Poems 1972–1977* (1978); and *White Shroud: Poems 1980–1985* (1986).

In June 1965, consorting with "hardened" rock musicians and in kinship with the Byrds, Dylan recorded his most ascendant song yet, "Like a Rolling Stone." Devoid of obvious protest references, set against a rough-hewn, twangy rock underpinning, and fronted by a snarling vocal that lashed out at all those who questioned his legitimacy, "Like a Rolling Stone" spoke to yet a new set of listeners and reached number two on the popular music charts. It was the final link in the chain. The world fell at Dylan's feet. And the album containing the hit single, *Highway 61 Revisited*, further vindicated his abdication of the protest throne.

THAT WILD MERCURY SOUND: DYLAN'S ROCK-AND-ROLL TARGET

At the 1965 Newport Folk Festival, Dylan bravely showcased his electric sound, backed primarily by the Paul Butterfield Blues Band. After a short 15-minute set, Dylan left the stage to a hail of booing—most likely either as response to the headliner's unexpectedly abbreviated performance or to his electrification. He returned for a two-song acoustic encore. Reams were written about his electric betrayal and banishment from the folk circle. By the time of his next public appearance, at the Forest Hills (New York) Tennis Stadium a month later, the audience had been "instructed" by the press how to react. After a well-received acoustic opening set, Dylan was joined by his new backing band (Al Kooper on keyboards, Harvey Brooks on bass, and, from the Hawks, Canadian guitarist Robbie Robertson and drummer Levon Helm). Dylan and the band were booed throughout the performance; incongruously, the audience sang along with "Like a Rolling

DYLAN GOES ELECTRIC

Bob Dylan's performance at the Newport Folk Festival in 1965 is widely regarded as one of the pivotal moments in the history of rock music. But, if there is near consensus on its importance, there is much less agreement on exactly what happened. Rock historians, Dylan's biographers, and eyewitnesses provide varying accounts of the audience's reaction to Dylan's performance, the reasons behind those reactions, and Dylan's response.

This much is clear: when Dylan took the stage at Newport on July 25, 1965, he was the leading light of the folk music revival of the early 1960s. The pursuit of "authenticity" lay at the heart of the revival, and as such it was generally believed that real folk music was played only on acoustic instruments. Folk purists had little respect for rock and roll, which most regarded as puerile and crassly commercial. In the months leading up to Newport, Dylan, theretofore the quintessential acoustic troubadour, had released the partly electric album *Bringing It All Back Home* and had recorded much of *Highway 61 Revisited* with rock-oriented musicians and electric instruments. The week of the 1965 festival, Dylan's acerbic single "Like a Rolling Stone" was omnipresent on U.S. Top 40 radio. Called electric blues by some and rock and roll by others, it was unquestionably not the folk music for which he was known.

Interested in duplicating this electric sound live at Newport, Dylan hastily recruited members of the Paul Butterfield Blues Band (guitarist Mike Bloomfield, drummer Sam Lay, and bassist Jerome Arnold), along with session pianist Barry Goldberg and keyboardist Al Kooper, who had created the signature organ sound on "Rolling Stone," to act as his backing band. They rehearsed deep into the night of July 24. Even before their set with Dylan, the Butterfield band had stirred controversy with their performance of electric blues during a festival workshop (at which Dylan's manager, Albert

Bob Dylan with a Fender Stratocaster electric guitar at the Newport Folk Festival in 1965. His performance unleashed a flurry of mixed reactions and dramatically changed the face of both folk and rock music. Alice Ochs/Michael Ochs Archives/Getty Images

Grossman, and folklorist Alan Lomax scuffled after Lomax's disparaging introduction of the Butterfield band) and earlier on July 25 with their performance on the main stage.

For his set, Dylan, brandishing a solid-body electric guitar, "plugged in" with the rest of the band. The set began with "Maggie's Farm" from *Highway 61.* This is where the accounts diverge. Some (notably critic and biographer Robert Shelton) reported that the audience immediately "registered hostility" and that boos and cat-calls ("Play folk music!" "Get rid of the band!") began at the end of "Maggie's Farm" and escalated through the next song, "Like a Rolling Stone." Dylan biographer Anthony Scaduto described the audience's initial reaction as a mixture of scattered booing and applause but mostly bewildered silence. According to Scaduto, booing and heckling then spread throughout the audience during "Rolling Stone," driving Dylan and the band offstage after the performance of a third song, an early version of "It Takes a Lot to

Laugh, It Takes a Train to Cry." Scaduto cited an interpretation of the event by folk musician Ric von Schmidt that has been echoed by others (notably biographer Bob Spitz, who also reported that some audience members booed as soon as they realized that amplified instruments were going to be used). According to von Schmidt, Dylan's voice was overwhelmed by the band as the result of poor sound mix (which most accounts describe as muddy or unbalanced at best), which led the people closest to the stage to call out that they couldn't make out Dylan's words ("Can't hear ya!" "Turn the sound down!"). The members of the audience who were farther back, said von Schmidt, misunderstood the complaints and responded with booing and jeering—probably based on the belief that Dylan was betraying folk music by going electric. What is certain is that there was booing (and cheering) and that after three songs Dylan and the band left the stage. According to Kooper, who was at Dylan's side onstage, the performers left because they had rehearsed only three songs, and the booing was primarily a response to the brevity of the set by the performer that most of the audience had come to hear.

There also are varying accounts of what transpired backstage during the performance, but it seems likely that a confrontation took place at the sound board between festival board members: Lomax and Pete Seeger wanted to cut the electricity; Grossman and Peter Yarrow (of Peter, Paul and Mary) successfully opposed them. There had already been a similar confrontation during the Butterfield band's performance earlier in the day. Dylan returned to the stage with an acoustic guitar (at Yarrow's behest, according to most accounts) and was greeted by thunderous applause. He performed "Mr. Tambourine Man" and "It's All Over Now Baby Blue," and as he did so, according to Greil Marcus in *Old Weird America* there were tears in Dylan's eyes. Scaduto, too, described the tears, and several accounts characterize Dylan as shaken and confused. Kooper, on the other hand, said there were no tears.

And so the debate lives on, decades after the event. But what no one denies is that folk and rock music were never the same after that memorable day at Newport in 1965.

Stone," the number two song in the United States that week, and then booed at its conclusion.

Backed by Robertson, Helm, and the rest of the Hawks (Rick Danko on bass, Richard Manuel on piano, and Garth Hudson on organ and saxophone), Dylan toured incessantly in 1965 and 1966, always playing to sold-out, agitated audiences. On November 22, 1965, Dylan married Sara Lowndes. They split their time between a townhouse in Greenwich Village and a country estate in Woodstock, New York.

In February 1966, at the suggestion of his new producer, Bob Johnston, Dylan recorded at Columbia's Nashville, Tennessee, studios, along with Kooper, Robertson, and the cream of Nashville's play-for-pay musicians. A week's worth of marathon 20-hour sessions produced a double album that was more polished than the raw, almost punklike *Highway 61 Revisited*. Containing some of Dylan's finest work, *Blonde on Blonde* peaked at number nine, was critically acclaimed, and pushed Dylan to the zenith of his popularity. He toured Europe with the Hawks (soon to reemerge as the Band) until the summer of 1966, when a motorcycle accident in Woodstock brought his amazing seven-year momentum to an abrupt halt. Citing a serious neck injury, he retreated to his home in Woodstock and virtually disappeared for two years.

During his recuperation, Dylan edited film footage from his 1966 European tour that was to be shown on television but instead surfaced years later as the seldom-screened film *Eat the Document*. In 1998 some of the audio recordings from the film, including portions of Dylan's performance at the Free Trade Hall in Manchester, England, were released as the album *Live 1966*.

In 1967 the Band moved to Woodstock to be closer to Dylan. Occasionally they coaxed him into the basement studio of their communal home to play music together, and recordings from these sessions ultimately became the double album *The Basement Tapes* (1975). In early 1968 Columbia released a stripped-down album of new Dylan songs titled *John Wesley Harding*. At least partly because of public curiosity about Dylan's seclusion, it reached number two on the pop album charts (eight places higher than *Bob Dylan's Greatest Hits*, released in 1967).

COUNTRY PIE

In January 1968 Dylan made his first post-accident appearance at a memorial concert for Woody Guthrie in New York City. His image had changed; with shorter hair, spectacles, and a neglected beard, he resembled a rabbinical student. At this point Dylan adopted the stance he held for the rest of his career: sidestepping the desires of the critics, he went in any direction but those called for in print. When his audience and critics were convinced that his muse had left him, Dylan would deliver an album at full strength, only to withdraw again.

Dylan returned to Tennessee to record *Nashville Skyline* (1969), which helped launch an entirely new genre, country rock. It charted at number three, but, owing to the comparative simplicity of its lyrics, people questioned whether Dylan remained a cutting-edge artist. Meanwhile, rock's first bootleg album, *The Great White Wonder*—containing unreleased, "liberated" Dylan recordings—appeared in independent record stores. Its distribution methods were shrouded in secrecy (certainly Columbia, whose contract with Dylan the album violated, was not involved).

Over the next quarter century Dylan continued to record, toured sporadically, and was widely honoured, though his impact was never as great or as immediate as it had been in the 1960s. In 1970 Princeton University (N.J.) awarded him an honorary doctorate of music. His first book, *Tarantula*, a collection of unconnected writings, met with critical indifference when it was unceremoniously published in 1971, five years after its completion. In August 1971 Dylan made a rare appearance at a benefit concert that former Beatle George Harrison had organized for the newly independent nation of Bangladesh. At the end of the year, Dylan purchased a house in Malibu, California; he had already left Woodstock for New York City in 1969.

In 1973 he appeared in director Sam Peckinpah's film *Pat Garrett and Billy the Kid* and contributed to the soundtrack, including "Knockin' on Heaven's Door." *Writings and Drawings*, an anthology of his lyrics and poetry, was published the next year. In 1974 he toured for the first time in eight years, reconvening with the Band (by this time popular artists in their own right). *Before the Flood*, the album documenting that tour, reached number three.

TANGLED UP IN BLUE

Released in January 1975, Dylan's next studio album, *Blood on the Tracks*, was a return to lyrical form. It topped the charts, as did *Desire*, released one year later. In 1975 and 1976 Dylan barnstormed North America with a gypsylike touring company, announcing shows in radio interviews only hours before appearing. Filmed and recorded, the

REPRESENTATIVE WORKS

- ▶ *The Freewheelin' Bob Dylan* (1963)
- ▶ *The Times They Are A-Changin'* (1964)
- ▶ *Another Side of Bob Dylan* (1964)
- ▶ *Bringing It All Back Home* (1965)
- ▶ *Highway 61 Revisited* (1965)
- ▶ *Blonde on Blonde* (1966)
- ▶ *John Wesley Harding* (1968)
- ▶ *Nashville Skyline* (1969)
- ▶ *New Morning* (1970)
- ▶ *Planet Waves* (1974)
- ▶ *Blood on the Tracks* (1975)
- ▶ *Desire* (1976)
- ▶ *Street-Legal* (1978)
- ▶ *Slow Train Coming* (1979)
- ▶ *The 30th Anniversary Concert Celebration* (1993)
- ▶ *MTV Unplugged* (1995)
- ▶ *Time Out of Mind* (1997)

Rolling Thunder Revue—including Joan Baez, Allen Ginsberg, Ramblin' Jack Elliott, and Roger McGuinn—came to motion-picture screens in 1978 as part of the four-hour-long, Dylan-edited *Renaldo and Clara*.

Lowndes and Dylan divorced in 1977. They had four children, including son Jakob, whose band, the Wallflowers, experienced pop success in the 1990s. Dylan was also stepfather to a child from Lowndes's previous marriage. In 1978 Dylan mounted a yearlong world tour and released a studio album, *Street-Legal*, and a live album, *Bob Dylan at Budokan*. In a dramatic turnabout, he converted to Christianity in 1979 and for three years recorded and performed only religious material, preaching between songs at live shows. Critics and listeners were, once again, confounded. Nonetheless, Dylan received a Grammy Award in 1980 for best male rock vocal performance with his "gospel" song "Gotta Serve Somebody."

By 1982, when Dylan was inducted into the Songwriters Hall of Fame, his open zeal for Christianity was waning. In 1985 he participated in the all-star charity recording "We Are the World," organized by Quincy Jones, and published his third book, *Lyrics: 1962–1985*. Dylan toured again in 1986–87, backed by Tom Petty and the Heartbreakers, and in 1987 he costarred in the film *Hearts of Fire*. A year later he was inducted into the Rock and Roll Hall of Fame, and the Traveling Wilburys (Dylan, Petty, Harrison, Jeff Lynne, and Roy Orbison) formed at his house in Malibu and released their first album.

THE ENDLESS TOUR

In 1989 Dylan once again returned to form with *Oh Mercy*, produced by Daniel Lanois. When *Life* magazine published a list of the 100 most influential Americans of the 20th century in 1990, Dylan was included, and in 1991 he received a Grammy Award for lifetime achievement. In 1992 Columbia Records celebrated the 30th anniversary of Dylan's

signing with a star-studded concert in New York City. Later this event was released as a double album and video. As part of Bill Clinton's inauguration as U.S. president in 1993, Dylan sang "Chimes of Freedom" in front of the Lincoln Memorial.

As the 1990s drew to a close, Dylan, who was called the greatest poet of the second half of the 20th century by Allen Ginsberg, performed for the pope at the Vatican, was nominated for the Nobel Prize for Literature, received the John F. Kennedy Center Honors Award, and was made Commander in the Order of Arts and Letters (the highest cultural award presented by the French government). In 1998, in a comeback of sorts, he won three Grammy Awards—including album of the year—for *Time Out of Mind*. In 2000 he was honoured with a Golden Globe and an Academy Award for best original song for "Things Have Changed," from the film *Wonder Boys*. Another Grammy (for best contemporary folk album) came Dylan's way in 2001, for *Love and Theft*.

In 2003 he cowrote and starred in the film *Masked & Anonymous* and, because of the effects of carpal tunnel syndrome, began playing electric piano exclusively in live appearances. The next year he released what portended to be the first in a series of autobiographies, *Chronicles: Volume 1*. In 2005 *No Direction Home*, a documentary directed by Martin Scorsese, appeared on television. Four hours long, yet covering Dylan's career only up to 1967, it was widely hailed by critics. A soundtrack album that included 26 previously unreleased tracks came out before the documentary aired. In 2006 Dylan turned his attention to satellite radio as the host of the weekly *Theme Time Radio Hour* and released his 44th album, *Modern Times*, which won the 2007 Grammy Award for best contemporary folk album. Dylan also received an award for best solo rock vocal performance for "Someday Baby."

In presenting to Dylan Spain's Prince of Asturias Prize for the Arts in 2007, the jury called him a "living myth in the history of popular music and a light for a generation that dreamed of changing the world," and in 2008 the Pulitzer Prize Board awarded him a special citation for his "profound impact on popular music and American culture." In 2009 Dylan, who was still actively performing in his late 60s, released his 33rd studio album, *Together Through Life*, which debuted at the top of the British and American album charts.

CHAPTER 8

Folk Rock

As the American folk music revival gathered momentum in the 1950s and '60s, it was inevitable that a high-minded movement that prided itself on the purity of its acoustic instrumentation and its separation from the commercial pop mainstream would be overtaken and transformed by pop music's rapidly evolving technology. Rock music also was transformed by its intersection with folk. Although rock previously had been perceived and created almost exclusively as entertainment, it now began to take on folk music's self-conscious seriousness of intent. The catalytic figure in the fusion of folk and commercial rock was Bob Dylan,

Dylan's going electric at Newport certified a fusion that had already taken place. The hybrid had been presaged in the late 1950s by the hugely popular college campus favourites the Kingston Trio. Two years before Dylan's notorious Newport appearance, which struck die-hard folk purists as a sellout, Peter, Paul and Mary had already reached number two in the charts with a homogenized pop rendition of Dylan's protest anthem "Blowin' in the Wind." Dylan's move, which followed the release of his partly electric album *Bringing It All Back Home* (1965), accelerated the already growing onslaught of socially conscious folk-flavoured music done with a rock beat and electric guitars.

THE BYRDS: BEATLIZED DYLANS

The genre reached a peak of formal elegance in the music of the Byrds, a Los Angeles-based quintet whose sound was constructed around the jangling chime of 12-string electric guitars and Beatles-influenced vocal harmonies. The principal members were Roger McGuinn (born James Joseph McGuinn III, July 13, 1942, Chicago, Illinois, U.S.), Gene Clark (born Harold Eugene Clark, November 17, 1941, Tipton, Missouri—died May 24, 1991, Sherman Oaks, California), David Crosby (born David Van Cortland, August 14, 1941, Los Angeles, California), Chris Hillman (born December 4, 1942, Los Angeles), Michael Clarke (born June 3, 1944, New York, New York—died December 19, 1993, Treasure Island, Florida), Gram Parsons (born Ingram Cecil Connor III, November 5, 1946, Winter Haven, Florida—died September 19, 1973, Yucca Valley, California), and Clarence White (born June 6, 1944, Lewiston, Maine—died July 14, 1973, Palmdale, California).

The Byrds' debut single, a version of Dylan's "Mr. Tambourine Man," went to number one in 1965, breaking the British Invasion's yearlong dominance of Top 40 airplay and record sales in the United States. They introduced Dylan's songwriting to a new, commercially empowered, teenage pop audience and, in the process, established Los Angeles as the creative hotbed of a new, "mod," distinctly American style of rock. The Byrds' trademark sound—a luminous blend of 12-string electric guitar and madrigal-flavoured vocal harmonies—spiked the Appalachian folk music tradition with the rhythmic vitality of the Beatles and the sunny hedonism of southern California. On early albums, the Byrds covered Dylan, Pete Seeger, Porter Wagoner, and Stephen Foster with a jangly clarity that reflected young America's changing mood and its fantasies of a Pacific Coast utopia.

Former folkies converted by Beatlemania, McGuinn (who was called Jim before changing his name to Roger later in his career), Clark, and Crosby founded the Byrds—initially as the Jet Set and the Beefeaters—in 1964. (McGuinn had been a member of the Chad Mitchell Trio and a sideman for Judy Collins; Clark had been a member of the New Christy Minstrels.) But the Byrds brought new, formidable influences to folk and pop. Crosby's interest in modern jazz and Indian ragas inspired the Byrds' forays into modal psychedelia, including the hit "Eight Miles High" (1966). Hillman, a teenage mandolin prodigy, was a prime, underacknowledged force in the Byrds' fusion of rock and country.

In his songs "Mr. Spaceman" and "5D (Fifth Dimension)," McGuinn, an aviation and technology enthusiast, charged the Byrds' music and image with space-age optimism; he was also one of the first pop musicians to embrace the Moog synthesizer.

Formed more out of common ambition than fraternal bonding, the Byrds were racked by dissent. Clark, a prolific writer of melodically imaginative, bittersweet ballads, left in 1966; Crosby was fired in 1967 during the making of *The Notorious Byrd Brothers* (1968). Parsons, who had attempted a country-rock marriage with his previous group, the International Submarine Band, was a Byrd for only five months in 1968. Nevertheless, Parsons's Southern background and his passion for rural American music, including gospel and rhythm and blues, deeply informed the country sound of *Sweetheart of the Rodeo*, a record so controversial it alienated the Byrds' pop audience at the same time it outraged the Nashville music establishment (although the group did perform on the Grand Ole Opry radio program in 1968).

In the late 1960s and early '70s the Byrds were as famous for their influence and the activities of their alumni as for their actual recordings. The Byrds' blending of folk, country, and psychedelia was recast and commercially fine-tuned by bands such as Buffalo Springfield, Poco, and the Eagles. Hillman left the Byrds shortly after Parsons; together they founded the seminal country rock band the Flying Burrito Brothers. Crosby produced Joni Mitchell's first album, collaborated with members of the Grateful Dead and Jefferson Airplane, and, with Stephen Stills of Buffalo Springfield and the Hollies' Graham Nash, formed the "super-trio" Crosby, Stills and Nash (which became a quartet with the occasional addition of Neil Young). The Byrds' legacy was revived in the 1980s, as an earthy antidote to punk nihilism and synthesizer-driven pop, by the American underground bands R.E.M. and the Long Ryders. In the 1990s the Byrds' progressive country aspirations inspired the alternative country movement led by Wilco and Son Volt.

With a shifting lineup, the Byrds remained a popular act until 1973, when McGuinn, the sole remaining founding member, went solo. Clarence White, an experienced session musician who played with the bluegrass group the Kentucky Colonels, brought an exhilirating, concise style of roots rock guitar to later Byrds albums. There were periodic reunions by members of the original lineup during the 1970s, including a 1973 album by the full quintet. The 1990 boxed set *The Byrds* featured four new recordings by McGuinn, Crosby, and Hillman, one of which was, appropriately, a Bob Dylan song, "Paths of Victory." The Byrds were inducted into the Rock and Roll Hall of Fame in 1991.

EXPECTING TO FLY: OTHER AMERICAN FOLK ROCKERS

As folk rock became the trend of the moment, however, its socially critical stance was quickly broadened and diluted, and the relationship between the music and its traditional sources became more tenuous, a matter more of "feeling" than of strict reverence for the past. In the United States folk rock acts like the Mamas & the Papas, Buffalo Springfield, the Lovin' Spoonful, Sonny and Cher, Simon and Garfunkel, and Janis Ian personified a generalized, often self-righteous youthful rebellion that in its more pointed songs was labeled "protest" music. The era's quintessential—although far from best—folk rock anthem was Barry McGuire's "Eve of Destruction," a haranguing list of social injustices strung around a vague apocalyptic warning, which reached number one in September 1965. Simon and Garfunkel's "The Sounds of Silence" (number one in January 1966) delivered a similarly ominous blanket warning in a softer, more poetic style.

SIMON AND GARFUNKEL

As teenagers in Queens, New York, Paul Simon (born October 13, 1941, Newark, New Jersey, U.S.) and Art Garfunkel (born November 5, 1941, New York, New York) teamed up to sing as a duo first known as Tom and Jerry. They had a modest hit (number 49 on the Billboard pop chart) in 1958 with "Hey Schoolgirl," which earned them an appearance on television's American Bandstand. Garfunkel also released a few records as solo artist Arty Garr in the early 1960s, but after high school, when the duo's follow-up records failed to gain success, Tom and Jerry went their separate ways. Both went on to college—Garfunkel to study architecture and mathematics at Columbia University, Simon to study English at Queens College, though he spent much of his time writing songs and continued recording under a number of different names. Simon went on to attend law school but dropped out, and he and Garfunkel began working together again. As Simon and Garfunkel they recorded an acoustic album in 1964, but split again, with Simon traveling to London, where he performed solo. When their album, *Wednesday Morning, 3 A.M.*, began to gain interest, Simon returned to the United States and the duo reunited.

Art Garfunkel (left) *and Paul Simon in a recording studio at Columbia Records.* Douglas R. Gilbert/Redferns/Getty Images

Beginning with "The Sounds of Silence," they became the most popular folk-pop duo of the 1960s and the musical darlings of literary-minded college-age baby boomers. In 1967 their music was a key ingredient in the success of the hit film *The Graduate*, and in 1970 they reached their zenith with Simon's inspirational gospel-flavoured anthem "Bridge over Troubled Water," which showcased Garfunkel's soaring, semi-operatic tenor.

From his first big hits, Simon aspired to a self-consciously elevated poetic tone in his lyric writing that was the antithesis of rock-and-roll spontaneity. Infatuated with teen-age street music in the mid-1950s, he returned throughout his career to the wellspring of dreamy doo-wop vocal harmony for inspiration and refreshment. His best early songs tend to be bookish, angst-ridden reveries with simple folk rock melodies and earnest, poetically ambitious (but often mannered) lyrics, some influenced by Bob Dylan. Simon's best narrative song from this period, "The Boxer" (1969), is the streamlined dramatic monologue of a down-and-out prize-fighter. Simon's fascination with pop vocal sound quickly expanded to include the sparkle of English folk music, the ethereal pipes and voices of Andean mountain music, and the arching passion of gospel.

After he and Garfunkel broke up in 1970 (they reunited briefly in the early 1980s for a tour and a live album), Simon pursued a successful career as a singer-songwriter of whimsical, introspective songs with tricky time signatures. His biggest solo success came in 1975 with *Still Crazy After All These Years*, a collection of wistful ruminations on approaching middle age.

When his popularity began to ebb, Simon jumped on the emerging world-music bandwagon. On a visit to South Africa, he met many of the musicians with whom he made *Graceland* (1986), an exquisite, multifaceted fusion of his own sophisticated stream-of-consciousness poetry with black South Africa's doo-wop-influenced "township jive" and Zulu choral music. Although some accused him of cultural thievery—i.e., the appropriation and exploitation of another culture's music—the album was one of the most critically acclaimed and commercially successful of the decade and helped put South African music on the world stage.

Simon made a similar pilgrimage to Brazil to record *Rhythm of the Saints* (1990), an even denser (and somewhat less popular) fusion of African-derived percussion with American folk rock. Its quirky non-linear lyrics were indebted to the language of the Nobel Prize-winning

COLUMBIA RECORDS: FOLK-ROCK FULCRUM

Columbia was the slowest of the major labels to realize that the youth market was not going to disappear, but by the end of the 1960s it had become the most aggressive company in pursuing that audience. Having previously had no substantial rock-and-roll star (apart from belatedly signing Dion at the end of 1962), Columbia—through a mixture of luck and foresight—wound up with three of the main folk-rock acts of the mid-1960s: Bob Dylan, the Byrds, and Simon and Garfunkel.

Veteran artists-and-repertoire man John Hammond had signed Dylan as a folksinger in 1961, but it was in-house producer Tom Wilson who produced the turning-point electric single "Like a Rolling Stone" in 1965 and who overdubbed drums and bass on Simon and Garfunkel's previously released "The Sound of Silence," transforming an album track into a hit single. Wilson went on to produce the Mothers of Invention and the Velvet Underground for MGM's Verve label, while Bob Johnston took over supervision of the rest of Dylan's groundbreaking albums for Columbia, surprising some by recording at Columbia's Nashville studios.

Out in Los Angeles, Terry Melcher produced the Byrds' chart-topping version of Dylan's "Mr. Tambourine Man." The song launched the West Coast's version of folk rock, which culminated in the Monterey Pop Festival in 1967, where Columbia's new managing director, Clive Davis, proved willing to pay more than anyone else for new performers. By no means did all his signings recoup their advances, but the success of Albert Grossman's protégé Janis Joplin meant that paying large advances became the new way to do business.

Caribbean poet Derek Walcott. Walcott became Simon's collaborator on *The Capeman*, Simon's first Broadway musical, which opened in January 1998 and was a critical and commercial failure. Based on a highly publicized 1959 New York City murder involving a Puerto Rican street gang, *The Capeman* featured a score by Simon (Walcott collaborated on the lyrics) that was a theatrical elaboration of the New York street music that had originally inspired him. But it also emphasized the long-underappreciated Hispanic contribution to urban pop.

In 1999 Simon teamed with Bob Dylan for a summer tour in the United States. The concert series, which ended Simon's eight-year absence from the road, marked the first time the two performers formally worked together. Later that year Simon continued on a solo tour, and in 2000 released *You're the One*, an understated and introspective album that was a departure from the expansive sound of *Graceland* and *Rhythm of the Saints*.

Simon continued to integrate new influences into his work, and he enlisted electronic music legend Brian Eno for *Surprise* (2006). In addition to cowriting three of the songs on *Surprise*, Eno was credited with creating the album's "sonic landscape"—a rich layering of electronic instrumentation and rhythms that complemented Simon's lyrics. Simon followed with *So Beautiful or So What* (2011), an album that was billed as a return to traditional songwriting. If *Still Crazy After All These Years* was a thirty-something's commentary on middle age, *So Beautiful or So What* was a meditation on mortality by an artist approaching his 70th birthday. Stylistically, it was something of a career retrospective, incorporating the story-song lyricism of the Simon and Garfunkel years, the African sounds of *Graceland*, and the pop sensibility with which he had always flirted.

Among songwriters of his generation, Simon enjoyed one of the longest-lasting careers as a pop innovator. Searching out and exploring the sounds of indigenous musical cultures, from Southern gospel to Brazilian and West African percussion, he integrated them into American rock and folk styles to create a highly flexible, personalized style of world music that was at once primitive and elegant. Simon and Garfunkel were inducted into the Rock and Roll Hall of Fame in 1990 and Simon on his own in 2001.

LOU ADLER AND THE MAMAS & THE PAPAS

Although he lacked the signature sound of Phil Spector or Brian Wilson, Lou Adler was an important

THE MONTEREY POP FESTIVAL

Held in Monterey, California, on June 16–18, 1967, the Monterey Pop Festival was the first commercial American rock festival. Dunhill Records executive Lou Adler and John Phillips of the Mamas & the Papas organized the festival around the concept of the successful Monterey Jazz Festival and staged it at that festival's site. Featuring the first major American appearances of Jimi Hendrix and the Who, it also introduced Janis Joplin to a large audience and featured performances by the Jefferson Airplane, the Grateful Dead, the Byrds, Canned Heat, Buffalo Springfield, Otis Redding, Ravi Shankar, and many others.

The timing of the festival was fortuitous: major record companies had just become aware of the commercial potential of the new rock music, and, as one witness said, "The action wasn't on the stage; it was at the bar, where the record companies and the managers were in a heated bidding war." The Who, Joplin, Hendrix, and the short-lived Electric Flag signed major record deals; Redding was introduced to a white audience; and the counterculture's music gained new legitimacy, all as a result of the Monterey Pop Festival. Filmed by D.A. Pennebaker and recorded (although contractual problems kept the album that documented the event under wraps for two decades), the festival was thought to have been very successful. However, a 1968 festival was scrapped when it was discovered that the proceeds and the festival company's bookkeeper had vanished.

catalyst for the new folk-rock sound of California. After working with Herb Alpert as a songwriter, producer, and artist manager at Keen and Dore Records in the late 1950s, Adler became West Coast promotion man and song-plugger for Don Kirshner's New York City-based Aldon Music. In that capacity he worked closely with Jan and Dean, and in 1964 he conceived and produced a very successful live album of "oldies" by Johnny Rivers.

In 1964 he formed Dunhill as a production outlet for songs by writers who included Steve Barri and P.F. Sloan. A year later Adler launched Dunhill as a label and topped the chart with "Eve of Destruction," written by Sloan and sung by Barry McGuire in a pastiche of Bob Dylan's style. Three Dog Night and the Grass Roots were regular hit-makers, but the Mamas & the Papas became Dunhill's flagship act. In 1967 the group's leader, John Phillips, worked alongside Adler to celebrate the emergent West Coast music scene at the Monterey Pop Festival.

Intricate harmonies brought the Mamas & the Papas to the forefront of the folk-rock movement. Veterans of the Greenwich Village folk scene, "Mama" Cass Elliot (born Ellen Naomi Cohen, September 19, 1943, Baltimore, Maryland, U.S.—died July 29, 1974, London, England), and Dennis Doherty (born November 29, 1941, Halifax, Nova Scotia, Canada—d. January 19, 2007, Mississauga, Ontario) performed in the Mugwumps with future members of the Lovin' Spoonful before joining husband and wife John Phillips (born August 30, 1935, Parris Island, South Carolina—died March 18, 2001, Los Angeles, California) and Michelle Phillips (born Holly Michelle Gilliam,

April 6, 1944, Long Beach, California) and relocating to Los Angeles in 1965 as the Mamas & the Papas.

At Dunhill, working with Adler, they tallied a series of hits with well-written songs, mostly by John Phillips, that proved perfect vehicles for the group's cascading harmonies, among them "California Dreamin'" (1965), "Monday, Monday" (1966), and "Creeque Alley" (1967). In sound and look the Mamas & the Papas typified the groovy optimism of the emerging hippie movement (John Phillips wrote "San Francisco [Be Sure to Wear Flowers in Your Hair]" for Scott McKenzie). One year after the Monterey Pop Festival, the group disbanded, re-forming briefly in 1971. Elliot, who became a soloist, died prematurely. The Phillipses divorced; Michelle became an actress, John eventually triumphed over drug addiction, and both wrote autobiographies, *California Dreamin'* (1986) and *Papa John* (1986), respectively. The group, which re-formed again with some new members in the 1980s, was inducted into the Rock and Roll Hall of Fame in 1998.

BUFFALO SPRINGFIELD

The Canadian-American band Buffalo Springfield combined inventive songwriting, skillful instrumental interplay, and harmony vocals into a stunning folk-rock signature sound

KHJ, "BOSS RADIO"

Los Angeles' KHJ, better known as "Boss Radio" in the mid-1960s, was the most imitated station of its time. After years of "personality" radio—dominated by deejay chatter and replete with long jingles— it ushered in the mainstreaming of Top 40 radio. Its designer, Bill Drake, a Georgia-born deejay, liked to keep things simple. As a budding programming consultant, he proved himself at three California stations (in Fresno, Stockton, and San Diego), succeeding with his formula of more music, less talk, shorter jingles, and the strategic placement of news, commercials, and other items that might cause listeners to tune out.

The RKO chain, Drake's employer in San Diego, then gave him a real challenge: KHJ, a moribund station playing middle-of-the-road music and ranking 15th in the Los Angeles market. Drake hired the witty Robert W. Morgan from KEWB in Oakland, California, to work mornings; Morgan suggested fellow deejay The Real Don Steele for the afternoon drive-time shift; and, for program director, Drake brought in the energetic and creative Ron Jacobs, who had given Drake a run for his ratings in Fresno. KHJ soared to the top within six months, and Drake and his partner, Gene Chenault, began spreading the formula to other RKO stations. Programmers around the country taped KHJ and emulated its format, although most of them did it poorly. It was not only radio people who revered KHJ; artists respected its power as well. One night in 1966, Brian Wilson of the Beach Boys telephoned KHJ to ask if the station wanted to play a recording he had just completed. He then brought a tape to the station's studios on Melrose Avenue, next to Paramount Studios, and KHJ became the first station to play "Good Vibrations."

that laid the groundwork for southern California country rock. Bursting with talent, the group formed in 1966 following a fortuitous encounter in a Los Angeles traffic jam between Stephen Stills (born January 3, 1945, Dallas, Texas, U.S.) and Richie Furay (born May 9, 1944, Yellow Springs, Ohio)—both veterans of the Greenwich Village folk scene—and Neil Young (born November 12, 1945, Toronto, Ontario, Canada), Dewey Martin (born September 30, 1942, Chesterville, Ontario—found dead February 1, 2009, Van Nuys, California), and Bruce Palmer (born 1946, Liverpool, Nova Scotia, Canada—died October 1, 2004, Belleville, Ontario), Canadians drawn to the "hip" epicentre of the burgeoning folk rock movement.

Furay, Stills, and Young all wrote songs, provided lead vocals, and played guitar. Palmer played bass; drummer Martin had played with country-rock pioneers the Dillards. In a six-week gig at the Whisky-A-Go-Go club on Sunset Strip, the band polished their sound and refined their image, later gaining a record label—Atlantic subsidiary Atco. Their biggest hit, "For What It's Worth" (1967), about clashes between youth and police on the Sunset Strip, remains evocative of the era's spirit and its tensions.

The group broke up in 1968, but post-breakup success came to Furay and Jim Messina (born December 5, 1947, Maywood, California), who had joined the group earlier in the year, in Poco; to Messina in Loggins and Messina; to Young in a prodigious solo career; and to Stills in Crosby, Stills and Nash, which at times also included Young. Buffalo Springfield was inducted into the Rock and Roll Hall of Fame in 1997.

THE LOVIN' SPOONFUL

Formed in 1965 in Greenwich Village, the Lovin' Spoonful crafted a "good-time" sound and cartoonish image. Their version of folk rock—combining skilled musicianship, zaniness, and blues and jug-band influences (related to the skiffle music that played an important role in the development of British rock and roll)—produced seven Top Ten singles. The first, "Do You Believe in Magic?" (1965), celebrated music's liberating power, as did "Nashville Cats" (1966). Other hits included gentle ruminations on romance "You Didn't Have to Be So Nice" (1965), "Daydream" (1966), and "Did You Ever Have to Make Up Your Mind?" (1966), along with the uncharacteristically boisterous "Summer in the City" (1966). Chief songwriter John Sebastian (born March 17, 1944, New York, New York, U.S.), who added lead vocals, guitar, harmonica, and autoharp, and lead guitarist Zal Yanovsky (born December 19, 1944, Toronto, Ontario, Canada—d. December 13, 2002, Kingston, Ontario) came from a folk background. Bassist Steve Boone (born September 23, 1943, Camp Lejeune, North Carolina) and drummer Joe Butler (born September 16, 1941, Glen Cove, New York) had played rock and roll. Later members included Jerry Yester (born January 9, 1943, Birmingham, Alabama).

Before disbanding in 1969, they recorded five albums plus two movie soundtracks. Yanovsky left the band in 1967 after controversy resulted from an arrest for possession of marijuana; Sebastian followed in 1968, distinguishing himself as a soloist with his engaging performance at Woodstock and the chart-topping single "Welcome Back" (1976), the theme song of the television series *Welcome Back, Kotter*. The Lovin' Spoonful, minus Yanovsky and Sebastian, reunited in the 1990s to play live and in 1999 released *Live at the Hotel Seville*. The group was inducted into the Rock and Roll Hall of Fame in 2000.

SONNY AND CHER

Sonny and Cher had their first big pop hit in 1965 with "I Got You Babe," which sold more than three million copies. Sonny Bono (born Salvatore Bono, February 16, 1935, Detroit, Michigan—died January 5, 1998, South Lake Tahoe, California) had moved to California in the early 1950s and began trying to sell his songs. After working in a succession of blue-collar jobs, he became a record packer at Specialty Records, where he worked his way up to writer and producer. He released a few records under a variety of pseudonyms and was co-writer (1962) of "Needles and Pins," which became a hit for Jackie DeShannon and later for the Searchers, before meeting (1963) and marrying (1964) Cher (born Cherilyn Sarkisian May 20, 1946, El Centro, California). The couple began recording Bono's songs in 1964 and hit gold a year later with "I Got You Babe." The duo went on to score a number of hits, but by the late 1960s their popularity had begun to fade. A jump-start came in 1971 with the television variety show *The Sonny and Cher Comedy Hour*, which ran until 1974. During this time Cher's solo singing career flourished. Cher and Sonny divorced in 1974, though they appeared as cohosts of another television show in 1976–77.

Cher appeared in the Broadway and film versions of *Come Back to the Five and Dime, Jimmy Dean, Jimmy Dean* (1982) and, turning increasing to film acting, received an Academy Award nomination for her performance in *Silkwood* (1983) and won an Oscar for her work in *Moonstruck* (1987). After two successful albums—

THE MONKEES

Motown's special case aside, the Monkees may have been the ulti-mate refutation of the 1960s rock audience's folk-derived precepts of authenticity. When the quartet was picked from more than 400 audition applicants to play a frolicsome ersatz Fab Four in an American television series (*The Monkees*) broadcast from 1966 to 1968, only folk rocker Mike Nesmith (born Robert Michael Nesmith, December 30, 1942, Houston, Texas, U.S.), who had some ability as a songwriter, and sometime folksinger Peter Tork (born Peter Thorkelson, February 13, 1942, Washington, D.C.), who had a nice smile, could claim musical experience. Davy Jones (born December 30, 1945, Manchester, England—died February 29, 2012, Stuart, Florida), the diminutive token Britisher who did double duty as "the cute one," was an ex-jockey but had been nominated for a Tony Award as best supporting actor in 1963 for *Oliver!*. Mickey Dolenz (born George Michael Dolenz, March 8, 1945, Los Angeles, California) was a former child actor who had starred in the late 1950s television series *Circus Boy*. Anonymous studio musicians supplied the backing on the "group's" records until the foursome, hoping to gain respectability, pushed for and got autonomy (includ-ing the opportunity to actually play their instruments) on the third Monkees album, *Headquarters* (1967).

However synthetic the premise or cynical the inspiration, their rich crop of Top 40 singles written to order by crack tunesmiths (including the teams of Gerry Goffin–Carole King and Tommy Boyce–Bobby Hart) remains 1960s pop at its tunefully rambunc-tious best, with the Neil Diamond-written, Dolenz-sung "I'm a Believer" standing as the group's—certainly Dolenz's and quite possibly Diamond's—finest hour. Since the late 1980s Dolenz, Jones, and Tork, occasionally joined by Nesmith but more often not, periodically cashed in on baby boomer nostalgia via tours, sporadic TV ventures, and a 1996 reunion album, with predictably negligible if also irrelevant artistic results. A series of tour dates in 2011 commemorated the 45th anniversary of the group's inception.

Cher (1987) and *Heart of Stone* (1989)—Cher's music career waned, but she made a comeback with *Believe* (1998) and *Living Proof* (2002). In 2000 she won a Grammy Award for the dance single "Believe." Bono went on to serve as the mayor of Palm Springs, California, and as a member of the House of Representatives before dying in a skiing accident.

THE TURTLES

Formed in Los Angeles in 1963 as a surf band, the Turtles underwent a series of name changes and passed through a British Invasion-influenced phase before registering their first hit single as folk rockers in 1965 with a version of Bob Dylan's "It Ain't Me Babe." Period gems, the Turtles' many hits included "You Baby" (1966), "She'd Rather Be with Me" (1967), "Happy Together" (1967), their biggest hit, and "Elenore" and "You Showed Me" from the ambitious 1968 album *The Turtles Present the Battle of the Bands*. The original members were Howard

Kaylan (born Howard Kaplan, June 22, 1947, New York, New York, U.S.), Mark Volman (born April 19, 1947, Los Angeles, California), Al Nichol (born March 31, 1946, Winston-Salem, North Carolina), Chuck Portz (born March 28, 1945, Santa Monica, California), and Don Murray (born November 8, 1945, Los Angeles—d. March 22, 1996, Santa Monica). At times musically adventurous, the Turtles experimented with psychedelic rock, exotica, odd time signatures, improvisations, theatrics, and satire. The band's core, vocalists Volman and Kaylan, continued as Flo (the Phlorescent Leech) and Eddie after the Turtles' dissolution in 1970, working with Frank Zappa, providing backup vocals for other performers—notably British glam rocker Marc Bolan's T. Rex—and recording and performing on their own.

THE BAND

Jaime ("Robbie") Robertson (born July 5, 1944, Toronto, Ontario, Canada),

Levon Helm (born May 26, 1940, Marvell, Arkansas, U.S.—died April 19, 2012, New York, New York), Rick Danko (born December 29, 1942, Simcoe, Ontario—died December 10, 1999, Marbletown, New York), Richard Manuel (born April 3, 1945, Stratford, Ontario—died March 4, 1986, Winter Park, Florida), and Garth Hudson (born August 2, 1937, London, Ontario) were five self-effacing sidemen pushed into becoming a self-contained group by Bob Dylan, the star in whose shadow they grew. As the Band they created a pioneering blend of traditional country, folk, old-time string band, blues, and rock music that brought them critical acclaim in the late 1960s and '70s and served as a template for Americana, the movement of hybrid, roots-oriented music that emerged in the late 1990s. Robertson was the group's principal writer and guitarist. Drummer Helm was a "good ol' boy" from Arkansas, the sole American in a lineup of displaced Canadians. Danko was the amiable hayseed on bass and occasional fiddle. Pianist Manuel sang blues ballads in a wrenching Ray Charles baritone. And Hudson's otherworldly keyboard doodles were the glue that held the whole operation together. At their peak, from 1968 to 1973, the quintet embodied better than any other group the sense of the American past that came to haunt pop culture after the hippie ideals of the 1960s had crashed to the ground.

The real midwife to the Band's birth was Ronnie Hawkins, a rockabilly diehard from Arkansas who ventured up to Canada in the spring of 1958. As Hawkins's lieutenant, Helm, still a teenager, helped recruit the young Ontarians—Robertson, Danko, Manuel, and Hudson—who replaced the original members of Hawkins's backing band, the Hawks. At a point when Fabian ruled the pop airwaves, the razorback rock and roll of the new Hawks was welcome only in the scuzziest roadhouses. During these years on the road, Robertson absorbed much of the flavour of life below the Mason and Dixon Line that would permeate Band songs like "The Night They Drove Old Dixie Down" (1969).

In 1964 the Hawks figured they could make it without Hawkins. During their summer residency on the New Jersey seaboard, Dylan got wind of their reputation and, after playing with Robertson, hired the group to back him on his first electric tour—a tour so controversial among folk purists that Helm could not take the pressure and quit. For the Hawks it was a baptism by fire, and it all but burned them out.

In 1967, in an effort to recuperate, the group (minus Helm) followed Dylan to Woodstock, New York. In nearby West Saugerties they gathered daily in the basement of "Big Pink," a secluded ranch house. Here the five men put together a rambling repertoire of old country, folk, and blues songs that later leaked out as a series of "basement tape" bootlegs and then as the double album *The Basement Tapes* (1975).

When Helm returned to the fold, Dylan began urging "the Band"—as they were now known locally—to go it alone. The immediate result of this separation was *Music from Big Pink* (1968), a wholly original fusion of country, gospel, rock, and rhythm and blues that, more than any other album of the period, signaled rock's retreat from psychedelic excess and blues bombast into something more soulful, rural, and reflective. Yet it was *The Band* (1969) that really defined the group's grainy character. Recorded in a makeshift studio in Los Angeles in early 1969, the album was a timeless distillation of American experience from the Civil War to the 1960s.

After the many years spent backing Hawkins and Dylan, the Band was ill-prepared for the vulnerability they felt singing their own songs onstage. After a disastrous debut at Winterland in San Francisco, they played to the massed tribes of the 1969 Woodstock festival. "We felt like a bunch of preacher boys looking into purgatory," recalled Robertson. This sense of alienation from the spirit of rock was reflected in *Stage Fright* (1970), an album full of foreboding and depression. Ironically, the record preceded the Band's most intensive period of touring, during which they became the formidable live unit of the magnificent *Rock of Ages* (1972).

The Band's experience on the road seemed to affect their confidence—particularly that of Robertson in his role as chief songwriter. Whereas *The Band* had sounded fresh and intuitive, *Cahoots* (1971) was laboured and didactic. After a mostly lost year in 1972, when Manuel's alcoholism became chronic, they trod water with *Moondog Matinee* (1973), an album of fine cover versions, then hitched their wagon once again to Dylan for the highly successful tour that produced *Before the Flood* (1974).

Just as they had followed Dylan to Woodstock, so the Band now decamped to southern California. The move suited Robertson, who acclimated quickly to the Hollywood lifestyle, but the others felt like fish out of water. *Northern Lights—Southern Cross* (1975) at least proved that the Band had not lost its keen musical empathy, but, when Robertson suggested dissolving the group after a final show at Winterland, he encountered little resistance.

Staged on Thanksgiving Day (November 25), 1976, this "Band and friends" finale was immortalized by Martin Scorsese's film *The Last Waltz*

(1978), with guest appearances by Dylan, Neil Young, and others. With only the lacklustre *Islands* (1977) as a last, contract-honouring memento of their career, the Band quickly fragmented. In 1983, sans Robertson, the group re-formed and played a less-than-spectacular tour. Three years later, Manuel was found hanging from a shower curtain in a Florida motel room.

Helm, Hudson, and Danko, who moved back to Woodstock, continued to operate as the Band and released three indifferent albums in the 1990s. Robertson remained in Los Angeles, where he made several solo albums and created film soundtracks. The Band was inducted into the Rock and Roll Hall of Fame in 1994.

CROSBY, STILLS AND NASH

With ex-members of three important 1960s rock groups—David Crosby (born David Van Cortland, August 14, 1941, Los Angeles, California, U.S.) from the Byrds, Stephen Stills (born January 3, 1945, Dallas, Texas, U.S.) from Buffalo Springfield, and Graham Nash (born February 2, 1942, Blackpool, Lancashire, England) from the Hollies—Crosby, Stills and Nash was the epitome of the supergroup (a group formed by already revered performers) when it formed in 1968. Capitalizing on the musicianship of gifted guitarist Stills, the skillful songwriting of all three members, and the dulcet three-part harmonies that were their trademark, Crosby, Stills and Nash produced a best-selling eponymous debut album in 1969 that remained on the charts for more than two years. With Young they turned out two number one albums, *Déjà vu* (1970) and the live *Four Way Street* (1971), before parting ways and re-forming for a concert tour in 1974, the same year that their compilation album, *So Far*, topped the charts. Ambition, ego, and internecine struggle led them to pursue solo careers, but they re-formed in various combinations in the following decades. Albums such as *American Dream* (1988) failed to exhibit the synergy of *Déjà vu*, sounding more like a collection of the various members' solo material than a collaborative effort. The group remained a successful live act into the 21st century, however, and consistently sold out venues around the world. Crosby, Stills and Nash was inducted into the Rock and Roll Hall of Fame in 1997.

WHO KNOWS WHERE THE TIME GOES?: FOLK ROCK IN BRITAIN

In Britain folk rock tended to be more respectful of tradition; groups like Fairport Convention, Pentangle, Steeleye Span (whose members included influential folksinger Martin

Carthy and vocalist Mandy Prior) and the Incredible String Band made records that combined centuries-old folk material with original, tradition-flavoured songs arranged for folk rock ensembles that often used old instruments to maintain a strong Celtic flavour.

FAIRPORT CONVENTION AND RICHARD THOMPSON

Fairport Convention's intermingling of traditional British folk songs, Bob Dylan obscurities, and haunting original compositions made the band a staple of folk rock in Britain. Along with the impassioned vocals of Sandy Denny (born January 6, 1947, Wimbeldon, England—died April 21, 1978) the intricate, stinging guitar playing of Richard Thompson (born April 3, 1949, London, England), gave Fairport Convention its rock edge. The fatalism of English folk ballads remained a hallmark of his songwriting.

Thompson left Fairport Convention in 1971 for a solo career, which soon became a partnership with his wife, Linda Thompson (born Linda Pettifer, 1948, Glasgow, Scotland). Their most notable albums together are *I Want to See the Bright Lights Tonight* (1974) and *Shoot Out the Lights* (1982). The latter documents a marital relationship in the last stages of deterioration; the Thompsons divorced soon after.

Thompson continued releasing solo albums, featuring as always his bitter but expert songwriting and dexterous guitar playing. He scored minor commercial successes with *Rumor and Sigh* (1991) and *Mock Tudor* (1999), and he toured regularly. When asked to assemble a list of the top 10 songs of the past millennium for a magazine article, Thompson took the assignment literally, collecting works that spanned from the 11th century to the 21st. Although his list was not printed, it inspired him to record *1000 Years of Popular Music* (2003), a compilation that traced the development of pop music from Early Middle English rounds to Britney Spears. Thompson reunited with the remaining members of Fairport Convention in 2007 for a celebration of the band's 40th anniversary.

PENTANGLE AND BERT JANSCH

Another of the leading figures in British folk music in the 1960s and early 1970s, both as a solo artist and as a member of the folk-rock group Pentangle, was guitarist, singer, and songwriter Bert Jansch (born November 3, 1943, Glasgow, Scotland—died October 5, 2011, Hampstead, London, England). Influenced by American folk-blues performers such as Big Bill Broonzy,

Jansch was part of the folk scene in Edinburgh, where he honed his skills as a guitarist before moving to London. Investing his playing style with baroque flourishes, he released several solo albums that featured both traditional material and original songs, including the highly regarded *Jack Orion* (1966). In 1967 he cofounded Pentangle, a folk-rock quintet that included another gifted guitarist, John Renbourn (with whom Jansch also collaborated outside the group), along with vocalist Jacqui McShee, bassist Danny Thompson, and drummer Terry Cox. Incorporating elements of jazz, blues, art rock, and traditional folk music (some dating to the Middle Ages), the band gained a cult following with the albums *Basket of Light* (1969) and *Cruel Sister* (1970), on the latter of which they briefly experimented with electric guitar.

Pentangle drifted apart in 1973 but re-formed with various lineups throughout the 1980s and '90s. In 2007 the original quintet took to the stage for the first time in more than 30 years when Pentangle was honoured with the BBC Radio 2 Folk Awards lifetime achievement award.

DONOVAN

In a more commercial vein, Donovan (born Donovan Phillip Leitch, May 10, 1946, Glasgow, Scotland) was a self-conscious answer to Dylan. Looking and sounding like Dylan, Donovan emerged in 1965 as a folksinger with "Catch the Wind." As the musical landscape became more kaleidoscopic, Donovan adapted his approach and helped define the era with odes to the hippie lifestyle such as "Sunshine Superman" (1966), "Mellow Yellow" (1967), and "Hurdy Gurdy Man" (1968). His obscure lyrics, often laced with drug references, were sung in a soft and sometimes soulful voice over melodies influenced by folk, blues, jazz, and Indian music. In the 1970s Donovan recorded several film soundtracks and continued to release albums sporadically into the 21st century. Notable recordings during this period were *Sutras* (1996), a folk album produced by Rick Rubin that recalled Donovan's earliest work, and *Beat Cafe* (2004), a lyrically clever collection that evoked the coffeehouse atmosphere of the Beat era. In 2011 Donovan was selected for induction into the Rock and Roll Hall of Fame.

VAN MORRISON

Irish singer-songwriter and occasional saxophonist Van Morrison (born George Ivan Morrison, August 31, 1945, Belfast, Northern Ireland) played in a succession of groups, most notably Them, in the mid-1960s before enjoying a long, varied,

Van Morrison performing in New York City. Michael Ochs Archives/Getty Images

and increasingly successful solo career. He is not easily categorized and could just as easily be lumped in with the singer-songwriters who would grow out of the folk-rock movement in the 1970s.

Morrison was born into a working-class Protestant family in Belfast. Having been exposed early to blues and jazz through his father's record collection and having taken up the saxophone, guitar, and harmonica, he began playing in bands while in his mid-teens. When he first appeared before British television audiences in 1965, fronting Them's thrilling rearrangement of an old blues song (Big Joe Williams's "Baby Please Don't Go"), it was clear that Morrison was different. Unlike his rivals, such as Mick Jagger or Eric Burdon, he seemed unwilling to flirt with the audience or even to make eye contact with them. The passion behind his harsh, stuttering delivery was obvious, but it seemed to be directed elsewhere.

More than anyone else, Morrison signaled the graduation of the rock singer from simple entertainer to something darker, more complex, and less susceptible to the music industry's mechanisms of control. He admired the integrity of the old bluesmen and the willfulness of poets, and his distaste for ingratiation provided a useful template for such later figures as Elvis Costello and John Mellencamp, who traded in related forms of surliness. It also won him a small but devoted following when it became apparent that, despite the success of "Brown Eyed Girl"—a snappy slice of uptown rhythm and blues that was his first solo single after leaving Them in 1967 and moving to the United States—the usual career yardsticks would not be applied. Indeed, that hit was never followed up. Instead, a year later he released *Astral Weeks*, an album of astonishing originality and inventiveness that stretched

the frontier of rock music. A cycle of extended semi-improvised songs with backing from an acoustic group including vibraharp, flute, guitar, bass, drums, and a small string section, it was neither rock nor folk nor jazz, and yet it was something of all three. Almost ignored at the time, it has come to be recognized as one of the most mesmerizingly intense and genuinely poetic works in the history of rock—not least for its classic track, the nine-minute "Madame George," in which Morrison achieves a sort of poetic trance wholly new to rock.

This mode, heavily influenced by the writings of John Donne, William Blake, and William Butler Yeats, was to come in for further investigation in "Listen to the Lion" (1972) and "Vanlose Stairway" (1982), but his future direction was more clearly indicated by *Moondance*, *Astral Weeks*'s successor, in which he deployed a snappy little rhythm-and-blues band behind tautly structured songs. The title song was the most obvious example, but it was followed over the years by such favourites as "Wild Night" and "Jackie Wilson Said" in pursuit of a style that was to affect the work of Tim Buckley and Bruce Springsteen, among others.

Moving between California, Ireland, and London, Morrison seemed oblivious to public taste and reaction to him. He pursued an interest in the music of his Celtic roots by collaborating with the Chieftains, developed his lifelong fondness for jazz with appearances at Ronnie Scott's Club in London, and wrote a series of songs in his own increasingly complex style that gave unmistakable evidence of a deep and unfulfilled spiritual yearning. Yet he was at his best onstage, where he could mix, match, and contrast all these approaches, indulging his love of the gifts of skilled musicians to his advantage and, no less, to theirs.

CHAPTER 9

The Times That Were Changing

The 1960s were marked by the greatest changes in morals and manners since the 1920s. Young people, college students in particular, rebelled against what they viewed as the repressed conformist society of their parents, and a countercultural movement that rejected the mores of mainstream American life originated on and around college campuses in the United States. Its members, called hippies, soon were found elsewhere, especially in Canada, Britain, and other western European countries. Their name was derived from "hip," a term often invoked by and used to describe the Beat Generation, the bohemian literary and social movement of the 1950s whose formative figures included Allen Ginsberg and Jack Kerouac. The youth-oriented counterculture of the 1960s and '70s evolved from two main strains, the social iconoclasm of the Beats and the political radicalism of the New Left. The latter, in turn, developed with the Free Speech and civil rights movements. The hippie movement arose in part in opposition to U.S. involvement in the Vietnam War; however, many hippies were not directly engaged in politics, and not all of those involved in the radical politics of the period considered themselves hippies. One group where the two strains met most directly and flamboyantly was the Youth International Party ("Yippies"), founded by Abbie Hoffman and Jerry Rubin.

THE NEW LEFT

The political activists of the New Left drew on the theories of political philosopher Herbert Marcuse, sociologist C. Wright Mills, and psychoanalyst and social philosopher Erich Fromm, among others. Founded in 1959, the Students for a Democratic Society (SDS) had its origins in the student branch of the League for Industrial Democracy, a social-democratic educational organization. Initially, SDS chapters throughout the country were involved in the civil rights movement. Operating under the principles of the "Port Huron Statement," a manifesto written by Tom Hayden and Robert Alan Haber and issued in 1962, the organization grew slowly until the escalation of U.S. involvement in Vietnam (1965), when it expanded quickly. SDS organized a national march on Washington, D.C., in April 1965, and, from about that period, SDS grew increasingly militant, especially about issues relating to the war, such as the drafting of students. Tactics included the occupation of university and college administration buildings on campuses across the country. By 1969 the organization had split into several factions, the most notorious of which was the "Weathermen," or "Weather Underground," which employed terrorist tactics in its activities.

THE CIVIL RIGHTS MOVEMENT

Following the U.S. Supreme Court decision in *Brown* v. *Board of Education of Topeka* (1954), African American and white supporters of civil rights attempted to end entrenched segregationist practices. When Rosa Parks was arrested in 1955 in Montgomery, Alabama, an African American boycott of the bus system was led by Martin Luther King, Jr., and Ralph Abernathy. In the early 1960s the Student Nonviolent Coordinating Committee (SNCC) led boycotts and sit-ins to desegregate many public facilities. Using the nonviolent methods of Mohandas K. Gandhi, the movement spread, forcing the desegregation of department stores, supermarkets, libraries, and movie theatres.

Another high point in the nonviolent struggle for civil rights came with the March on Washington in August 1963, when some 200,000 people gathered at the Lincoln Memorial in Washington, D.C., to hear King deliver his "I Have a Dream" speech. Earlier in the 1960s, extreme violence had greeted black and white Freedom Riders who had ridden together on interstate buses through the South in an attempt to prompt the federal government into enforcing its bans on segregation in

Dr. Martin Luther King, Jr., addressing a crowd of March on Washington demonstrators gathered on the National Mall in 1963. Hulton Archive/Getty Images

interstate bus travel and in bus terminals and facilities.

The passage of the Civil Rights Act of 1964 codified in federal law many of the goals of the civil rights movement; however, most African Americans in the South found it difficult to exercise the franchise. That year, SNCC, the Congress of Racial Equality (CORE), and the National Association for the Advancement of Colored People (NAACP) organized a massive effort to register voters in Mississippi. They also conducted classes on the philosophy of the civil rights movement, African American history, and leadership development. This "Freedom Summer" effort included a large number of white student activists from the North. When two white and one black volunteers were killed, it made headlines across the country, exponentially heightening awareness of the civil rights movement. On a small scale, these killings mirrored the violence experienced during the previous decade by countless African Americans—not only those who had participated in demonstrations but also many who had not—violence that ran from police beatings to the bombing of the homes, churches, and businesses of black people. Mass demonstrations were held in 1965 to protest the violence and other means used to prevent the registration of African American voters. Widespread indignation and anger in response to the halting by police violence of a peaceful protest march on the Edmund Pettus Bridge in Selma, Alabama, prodded Pres. Lyndon B. Johnson to push through the Voting Rights Act of 1965, which abolished literacy tests and other voter restrictions and authorized federal intervention against voter discrimination. Ultimately, politics in the South would be forever altered by the subsequent rise in black voter registration.

Yet despite the considerable gains of the civil rights movement, many African Americans were unhappy at the slow progress. The efficacy of the nonviolent methods of the movement was questioned by "Black power" advocates, such as Stokely Carmichael, who also challenged what they saw as the narrow goals of the civil rights movement and advocated instead a broader-based freedom struggle that sought wider political, economic, and cultural objectives. By the late 1960s King's Southern Christian Leadership Conference, the NAACP, SNCC, and CORE were all taken to task by militant organizations, such as the Black Panther Party. In most of the country's large cities, race riots erupted. Four years of summer violence in America's inner cities resulted in many deaths and widespread destruction that left whole neighbourhoods ruined. Following a final wave of violence provoked by the assassination of King in April 1968, the rioting abated. Yet African Americans remained undeterred in their activist pursuit of political and economic empowerment.

THE VIETNAM WAR

After the defeat of the French in the First Indochina War, Vietnam was partitioned so as to separate the warring parties until free elections could be held in 1956. Ho Chi Minh's popular—and communist-sympathizing—Viet Minh party from the North was expected to win the elections, which the leader in the South, Ngo Dinh Diem, refused to hold. In the war that ensued, fighters trained by North Vietnam (the Viet

Cong) fought a guerrilla war against U.S.-supported South Vietnamese forces; North Vietnamese forces later joined the fighting. At the height of U.S. involvement, there were more than half a million U.S. military personnel in Vietnam. The Tet Offensive of 1968, in which the Viet Cong and North Vietnamese attacked 36 of 44 South Vietnamese provincial capitals and 64 district capitals, marked a turning point in the war. Many in the U.S. had come to oppose the war on moral and practical grounds, and, as the antiwar movement swelled, President Johnson decided to shift to a policy of "de-escalation." Peace talks were begun in Paris. Between 1969 and 1973 U.S. troops were withdrawn from Vietnam, but the war was expanded to Cambodia and Laos in 1970. Ultimately as a result of peace talks that had reached a stalemate in 1971 but started again in 1973, a cease-fire agreement was reached. American involvement ended in 1975, with a defeat symbolized by the images of the frantic rooftop evacuation by helicopter of personnel of the U.S. embassy in Saigon.

1968

It is often argued that 1968 was the era's watershed year. The run-up to the 1968 election was transformed in 1967 when Minnesota's Democratic senator, Eugene J. McCarthy, challenged his party's leader, President Johnson, on his Vietnam War policies. Johnson had succeeded to the presidency in 1963, following the assassination of John F. Kennedy, and had been overwhelmingly reelected in 1964. Early in his term he was immensely popular, but, as the war's unpopularity mounted, so did Johnson's.

When Martin Luther King, Jr., was assassinated on April 4, 1968, in Memphis, Tennessee, profound shock among African Americans turned to anger, which found expression in rioting and violence in more than 100 cities, leading many white voters to look more closely at third-party candidate George Wallace, the former governor of Alabama, who was stressing "law and order" and promising to be on the ballot in 50 states. Then on June 4, Sen. Robert F. Kennedy, who had declared his candidacy for the presidency in March, scored a solid victory over McCarthy in California, but shortly after midnight, as the votes were still being counted, Kennedy was fatally shot.

The national conventions of the two parties could hardly have been more dissimilar. The Republicans convened amid the orderly opulence of Miami Beach, Florida, where the only hot question was whether New Yorker Nelson Rockefeller, California Gov. Ronald Reagan, and assorted favourite sons could stop Richard Nixon, who would eventually be

MEDIUM COOL

The movie *Medium Cool* follows television news cameraman John Cassellis (played by Robert Forster) as he shoots hard-to-get footage of disasters, accidents, and other unseemly incidents that his network demands. Cassellis faces a moral dilemma when he learns his bosses are providing footage to the Federal Bureau of Investigation to track down dissidents. Initially detached from the material he films, he experiences an emotional awakening by the movie's conclusion.

Scene from Medium Cool *(1969), directed by Haskell Wexler.* © 1969 Paramount Pictures Corporation and H & J Pictures, Inc. All rights reserved.

Made at the height of the Vietnam War protest movement, *Medium Cool* became controversial because of director and cinematographer Haskell Wexler's mixing of fact and fiction and his inclusion of actual footage he shot at the disastrous 1968 Democratic National Convention in Chicago. The film originally received an X rating, ostensibly because of its explicit language and nudity, but most critics felt the harsh rating stemmed from its counterculture subject matter. The film's title comes from Canadian communications scholar Marshall McLuhan's description of television as a "cool" medium.

the nominee and ultimately president. Security had been no problem for the Republican convention in Miami Beach, with the only disorder occurring miles away on the Florida mainland. But the Democrats, whose convention was in Chicago, were beset by organized plans to disrupt the convention proceedings within the hall and throughout the city. The Coalition for an Open Convention had brought about 1,200 dissenting Democrats to Chicago two months in advance in order to plan challenges to delegate credentials and also a platform repudiating the Democratic administration.

Throughout 1968, various peace groups—notably an amalgam of New Leftists, the National Mobilization Committee to End the War in Vietnam ("the Mobe" to its adherents), and the Youth International Party ("Yippies")—planned massive demonstrations. Before the Democratic convention opened, the demonstration leaders trained "parade marshals" in how to harass and penetrate police lines, in preparation for leading the expected scores of thousands of youthful demonstrators into confrontation with the police.

The threat of huge crowds of dissenters had put Chicago's nearly 12,000-man police force on 12-hour duty and brought some 13,000 National Guard and federal troops to the city. The harassment tactics—e.g., throwing rocks and bottles and using obscene language—precipitated recurring battles between demonstrators and police; many of the demonstrators were clubbed by the police as mayhem erupted. The most notorious scene took place on Wednesday night, August 28, when the organizers assembled their followers near the television cameras outside the convention headquarters hotel, the Conrad Hilton. Most of the 18-minute donnybrook touched off by brickbats, bottles, and bags hurled at police by agitators was caught on film, and the footage was shown on television throughout the country ("The whole world is watching," demonstrators chanted) for the rest of the week.

CULTURAL CHANGES IN BRITAIN

Beginning in the 1960s, pop music became an important area in which the identities of British young people were formed. Pop in Britain has modulated through many forms since then, from the punk of the late '70s and early '80s to hip-hop and the rave culture of the late 20th and early 21st century, and distinct styles of life have accreted around these musical forms, not only for youth. The development of a uniform popular culture, at least as expressed through popular music, was greatly beholden to similar developments in the United States, where social identities were explored and developed in terms of black popular music and

responses to it, not just by African Americans but also by young white Americans. Given the great importance of Afro-Caribbean immigration into Britain after 1945, and latterly South Asian immigration, the experience of ethnic minorities in Britain to some degree also paralleled that of the United States. Concerns about national identity, as well as personal and group identity, became more important as Britain became a multicultural society.

The civil rights movement in Ireland, student protest, and the anti-Vietnam War and civil rights movements in the United States were all part of the assault on the still-strong vestiges of Victorianism in British society, as well as, more immediately, a reaction against the austerity of postwar Britain. Change in family life and sexual mores was represented in the 1960s by a range of legislative developments, including the Abortion Act of 1967, the 1969 Divorce Reform Act, and the abolition of theatre censorship in 1968.

Change was also based on the relative economic affluence of the late 1950s and '60s. The disintegration of older values (including middle-class values) was evident in the "rediscovery" of the working class, in which films, novels, plays, and academic works depicted working-class life with unparalleled realism and unparalleled sympathy (including the works of the so-called Angry Young Men, various British novelists and playwrights who emerged in the 1950s and expressed scorn and disaffection with the established sociopolitical order of their country). The working class was therefore brought into the cultural mainstream. This was ironic at a time when working-class communities were in fact being broken apart by slum clearance and the relocation of populations away from the geographical locations of their traditional culture.

Changes in higher education, with the development of the polytechnics and the "new universities," meant that, at least to some extent, higher education was thrown open to children from poorer homes. There was also the liberalization of educational methods in primary and secondary education, along with the emergence of comprehensive schooling, ending the old distinction between the secondary modern and the grammar schools. In practice, many of the old divisions continued and, indeed, increased. However, rather than being accompanied by increasing cultural divisions, the opposite was the case. There was a much more positive understanding of the "popular" than before. A more fluid, open, and commercial popular culture was signalled by the development in the 1950s of commercial television and, with it, the slow decline of the public broadcasting, public service ethic of the BBC. Although these developments began to bring all classes together in a new demotic culture, differentiation according to income, taste, and education remained.

THE COUNTERCULTURE

In the 1960s in Britain, the United States, and elsewhere hippies felt alienated from middle-class society, which they saw as dominated by materialism and repression, and they developed their own distinctive lifestyle. They favoured long hair and casual, often unconventional, dress, including sandals, beads, bell-bottomed trousers, long, flowing dresses, and "granny" glasses. Hippies often lived communally or under cooperative arrangements, and they frequently adopted vegetarian diets and practiced holistic medicine. Many hippies "dropped out" from society, forgoing regular jobs and careers, although some developed small businesses that catered to the alternative lifestyles of hippies.

"Make love, not war" became the guiding aphorism for these "flower children." They coopted Winston Churchill's "V for victory" hand gesture and, by turning palm and fingers out, transformed it into the "peace sign." The hippies saw openness and tolerance as alternatives to what they viewed as the restrictions

EASY RIDER

Released in 1969, the film *Easy Rider* was hailed as a youth anthem for its message of nonconformism and its reflection of social tensions in the United States in the late 1960s. It helped spark the New Hollywood of the late 1960s and early '70s, in which a style of filmmaking based on low budgets and avant-garde directors—differing greatly from the traditional moviemaking of the Hollywood studios—arose.

Hippie drug dealers Wyatt (played by Peter Fonda, who also produced) and Billy (Dennis Hopper, who also directed) are ostensibly en route to New Orleans for Mardi Gras, but in reality they are on an odyssey in search of freedom and some meaning in life. Along the way they encounter an eclectic array of individuals, including George Hanson (Jack Nicholson), an establishment lawyer with a penchant for alcohol. The people they meet and the situations that follow represent the best and worst aspects of modern American life and reflect upon issues that were particularly popular with youth at that time, from the hippie and commune movement to racism, war, religious tolerance, and drug use.

Many of the scenes are crude and rambling—the film's original cut ran nearly four hours—and *Easy Rider* can easily be viewed as a period piece, albeit a significant one, that reflected simplistic, though common, perceptions of the day, with everything countercultural or mainstream deemed either good or evil, respectively. The film's bleak conclusion—in which Wyatt and Billy have a violent encounter with men in a pickup truck—is still jarring for audiences. The success of the low-budget film revolutionized filmmaking and hastened the end of the power wielded by the studio moguls in Hollywood. In addition, the film's use of popular rock songs in place of original music was a concept later adopted by other filmmakers.

and regimentation of middle-class society. Hippies often practiced open sexual relationships. Many of them sought spiritual guidance from sources outside the Judeo-Christian tradition, particularly in Eastern religions. Astrology was popular, and the period was often referred to as the Age of Aquarius. Hippies promoted the recreational use of hallucinogenic drugs, particularly marijuana and LSD (lysergic acid diethylamide), justifying the practice as a way of expanding consciousness.

Both folk and rock music were an integral part of hippie culture. The musical *Hair*, a celebration of the hippie lifestyle, opened on Broadway in 1968, and the film *Easy Rider*, which reflected hippie values and aesthetics, appeared in 1969.

Part music festivals, sometimes protests, and often simply excuses for celebrating life, public gatherings were an important part of the hippie movement. The first "be-in," called the Gathering of the Tribes, was held in San Francisco in 1967.

Attendees of the Woodstock Music and Art Fair of 1969 sit atop vans, cars, and buses. John Dominis/Time & Life Pictures/Getty Images

A three-day music festival known as the Woodstock Music and Art Fair, held in rural New York state in 1969, drew a huge audience and became virtually synonymous with the movement. Hippies participated in a number of teach-ins at colleges and universities in which opposition to the Vietnam War was explained, and they took part in antiwar protests and marches. They joined other protestors in the "moratorium"—nationwide demonstration—against the war in 1969. They were also involved in the development of the environmental movement.

WOODSTOCK

The most famous of the 1960s rock festivals, the Woodstock Music and Art Fair was held on a farm property in Bethel, New York, August 15–17, 1969. It was organized by four inexperienced promoters who nonetheless signed a who's who of current rock acts, including Jimi Hendrix, Sly and the Family Stone, the Who, the Grateful Dead, Janis Joplin, the Jefferson Airplane, Ravi Shankar, and Country Joe and the Fish.

The festival began to go wrong almost immediately, when the towns of both Woodstock and Wallkill, New York, denied permission to stage it. (Nevertheless, the name Woodstock was retained because of the cachet of hipness associated with the town, where Bob Dylan and several other musicians were known to live and which had been an artists' retreat since the turn of the century.) Ultimately, farmer Max Yasgur made his land available for the festival. Few tickets were sold, but some 400,000 people showed up, mostly demanding free entry, which they got due to virtually nonexistent security. Rain then turned the festival site into a sea of mud, but somehow the audience bonded—possibly because large amounts of marijuana and psychedelics were consumed—and the festival went on.

Although it featured memorable performances by Crosby, Stills and Nash (performing together in public for only the second time), Santana (whose fame at that point had not spread far beyond the San Francisco Bay area), Joe Cocker (then new to American audiences), and Hendrix, the festival left its promoters virtually bankrupt. They had, however, held onto the film and recording rights and more than made their money back when Michael Wadleigh's documentary film *Woodstock* (1970) became a smash hit. The legend of Woodstock's "Three Days of Peace and Music," as its advertising promised, became enshrined in American history. Many saw Woodstock as the apotheosis of the counterculture; many also, in retrospect, saw it as the beginning of the end.

CHAPTER 10

Soul Music

If rock and roll, represented by performers such as Elvis Presley, can be seen as a white reading of rhythm and blues, soul is a return to black music's roots—gospel and blues. The style is marked by searing vocal intensity, use of church-rooted call-and-response, and extravagant melisma. If in the 1950s Ray Charles was the first to secularize pure gospel songs, that transformation realized its full flowering in the work of Aretha Franklin, the "Queen of Soul," who, after six years of notable work on Columbia Records, began her glorious reign in 1967 with her first hits for Atlantic Records—"I Never Loved a Man (the Way I Love You)" and "Respect." Before Franklin, though, soul music had exploded largely through the work of Southern artists such as James Brown and Southern-oriented labels such as Stax/Volt.

The Motown Sound, which came of age in the 1960s, must also be considered soul music. In addition to its lighter, more pop-oriented artists such as the Supremes, the Motown label produced artists with genuine gospel grit—the Contours ("Do You Love Me" [1962]), Marvin Gaye ("Can I Get a Witness" [1963]), and Stevie Wonder ("Uptight [Everything's Alright]" [1966]). But Motown packaged its acts as clean-cut and acceptable, as it sought to sell to white teens. As the civil rights movement gained steam, black artists grew more politically aware. Rooted in personal expression, their music resonates with self-assertion, culminating in Brown's "Say It Loud—I'm Black and I'm Proud (Part 1)" (1968).

JAMES BROWN

James Brown (born May 3, 1933, Barnwell, South Carolina, U.S.—died December 25, 2006, Atlanta, Georgia) was raised mainly in Augusta, Georgia, by his great-aunt, who took him in at about the age of five when his parents divorced. Growing up in the segregated South during the Great Depression of the 1930s, Brown was so impoverished that he was sent home from grade school for "insufficient clothes," an experience that he never forgot and that perhaps explains his penchant as an adult for wearing ermine coats, velour jumpsuits, elaborate capes, and conspicuous gold jewelry. Neighbours taught him how to play drums, piano, and guitar, and he learned about gospel music in churches and at tent revivals, where preachers would scream, yell, stomp their feet, and fall to their knees during sermons to provoke responses from the congregation. Brown sang for his classmates and competed in local talent shows but initially thought more about a career in baseball or boxing than in music.

At age 15 Brown and some companions were arrested while breaking into cars. He was sentenced to 8 to 16 years of incarceration but was released after 3 years for good behaviour. While at the Alto Reform School, he formed a gospel group. Subsequently

secularized and renamed the Flames (later the Famous Flames), it soon attracted the attention of rhythm-and-blues and rock-and-roll shouter Little Richard, whose manager helped promote the group. Intrigued by their demo record, Ralph Bass, the artists-and-repertoire man for the King label, brought the group to Cincinnati, Ohio, to record for King Records's subsidiary Federal. The label's owner, Syd Nathan, hated Brown's first recording, "Please, Please, Please" (1956), but the record eventually sold three million copies and launched Brown's extraordinary career. Along with placing nearly 100 singles and almost 50 albums on the best-seller charts, Brown broke new ground with two of the first successful "live and in concert" albums—his landmark *Live at the Apollo* (1963), which stayed on the charts for 66 weeks, and his 1964 follow-up, *Pure Dynamite! Live at the Royal*, which charted for 22 weeks.

During the 1960s Brown was known as "Soul Brother Number One." His hit recordings of that decade have often been associated with the emergence of the Black Arts and black nationalist movements, especially the songs "Say It Loud—I'm Black and I'm Proud" (1968), "Don't Be a Drop-Out" (1966), and "I Don't Want Nobody to Give Me Nothin' (Open Up the Door, I'll Get It Myself)" (1969). Politicians recruited him to help calm cities struck by civil insurrection and avidly courted his endorsement. In the 1970s Brown became "the Godfather of Soul," and his hit songs stimulated several dance crazes and were featured on the soundtracks of a number of "blaxploitation" films (sensational, low-budget, action-oriented motion pictures with African American protagonists). When hip-hop emerged as a viable commercial music in the 1980s, Brown's songs again assumed centre stage as hip-hop disc jockeys frequently incorporated samples (audio snippets) from his records. He also appeared in several motion pictures, including *The Blues Brothers* (1980) and *Rocky IV* (1985), and attained global status as a celebrity, especially in Africa, where his tours attracted enormous crowds and generated a broad range of new musical fusions. Yet Brown's life continued to be marked by difficulties, including the tragic death of his third wife, charges of drug use, and a period of imprisonment for a 1988 high-speed highway chase in which he tried to escape pursuing police officers.

Brown's uncanny ability to "scream" on key, to sing soulful slow ballads as well as electrifying up-tempo tunes, to plumb the rhythmic possibilities of the human voice and instrumental accompaniment, and to blend blues, gospel, jazz, and country vocal styles together made him one of the most influential vocalists of the 20th century. His extraordinary dance routines featuring deft deployment of microphones and articles of clothing as props, acrobatic leaps, full-impact knee landings, complex rhythmic patterns, dazzling footwork, dramatic entrances, and melodramatic exits redefined public performance within popular music and inspired generations of imitators (not least Michael Jackson). His careful attention to every aspect of his shows, from arranging songs to supervising sidemen, from negotiating performance fees to selecting costumes, guaranteed his audiences a uniformly high level of professionalism every night and established a precedent in artistic autonomy, earning him the sobriquet "the Hardest-Working Man in Show Business." In the course of an extremely successful commercial career, Brown's name was associated with an extraordinary number and range of memorable songs, distinctive dance steps, formative fashion trends, and even significant social issues. A skilled dancer and singer with an extraordinary sense of timing, Brown played a major role in bringing rhythm to the foreground of popular music. In addition to providing melody and embellishment, the horn players in his bands functioned as a rhythm section (they had to think like drummers), and musicians associated with him (Jimmy

Nolan, Bootsy Collins, Fred Wesley, and Maceo Parker) have played an important role in creating the core vocabulary and grammar of funk music. Brown was inducted into the Rock and Roll Hall of Fame in 1986.

ARETHA FRANKLIN

Aretha Franklin (born March 25, 1942 Memphis, Tennessee, U.S.) defined the golden age of soul music of the 1960s. Her mother, Barbara, was a gospel singer and pianist. Her father, C.L. Franklin, presided over the New Bethel Baptist Church of Detroit, Michigan, and was a minister of national influence. A singer himself, he was noted for his brilliant sermons, many of which were recorded by Chess Records.

Her parents separated when she was six, and Franklin remained with her father in Detroit. Her mother died when Aretha was 10. As a young teen, Franklin performed with her father on his gospel programs in major cities throughout the country and was recognized as a vocal prodigy. Her central influence, Clara Ward of the renowned Ward Singers, was a family friend. Other gospel greats of the day—Albertina Walker and Jackie Verdell—helped shape young Franklin's style. Her album *The Gospel Sound of Aretha Franklin* (1956) captures the electricity of her performances as a 14-year-old.

At age 18, with her father's blessing, Franklin switched from sacred to secular music. She moved to New York City, where Columbia Records executive John Hammond, who had signed Count Basie and Billie Holiday, arranged her recording contract and supervised sessions highlighting her in a blues-jazz vein. From that first session, "Today I Sing the Blues" (1960) remains a classic. But, as her Detroit friends on the Motown label enjoyed hit after hit, Franklin struggled to achieve crossover success. Columbia placed her with a variety of producers who marketed her to both adults ("If Ever You Should Leave Me," 1963) and teens ("Soulville," 1964). Without targeting any particular genre, she sang everything from Broadway ballads to youth-oriented rhythm and blues. Critics recognized her talent, but the public remained lukewarm until 1966, when she switched to Atlantic Records, where producer Jerry Wexler allowed her to sculpt her own musical identity.

At Atlantic, Franklin returned to her gospel-blues roots, and the results were sensational. "I Never Loved a Man (the Way I Love You)" (1967), recorded at Fame Studios in Florence, Alabama, was her first million-seller. Surrounded by sympathetic musicians playing spontaneous arrangements and devising the background vocals herself, Franklin refined a style associated with Ray

Aretha Franklin playing the piano and singing during a recording session at Columbia Records. Frank Driggs Collection/Archive Photos/ Getty Images

Charles—a rousing mixture of gospel and rhythm and blues—and raised it to new heights. As a civil-rights-minded nation lent greater support to black urban music, Franklin was crowned the "Queen of Soul." "Respect," her 1967 cover of Otis Redding's spirited composition, became an anthem operating on personal, sexual, and racial levels. "Think" (1968), which Franklin wrote herself, also had more than one meaning. For the next half-dozen years, she became a hit maker of unprecedented proportions; she was "Lady Soul."

In the early 1970s she triumphed at the Fillmore West in San Francisco before an audience of flower children and on whirlwind tours of Europe and Latin America. Her return to church, *Amazing Grace* (1972), is considered one of the great gospel albums of any era. By the late 1970s disco cramped Franklin's style and eroded her popularity. But in 1982, with help from singer-songwriter-producer Luther Vandross, she was back on top with a new label, Arista, and a new dance hit, "Jump to It," followed by "Freeway of Love" (1985). A reluctant interviewee, Franklin kept her private life private, claiming that the popular perception associating her with the unhappiness of singers Bessie Smith and Billie Holiday was misinformed.

In 1987 Franklin became the first woman inducted into the Rock and Roll Hall of Fame. While her album sales in the 1990s and 2000s failed to approach the numbers of previous decades, Franklin remained the Queen of Soul, and in 2009 she electrified a crowd of more than one million with her performance at the presidential inauguration of Barack Obama.

STAX RECORDS

Stax/Volt Records in Memphis, Tennessee, was built on an unshakable foundation of straight-up soul. Singers such as Otis Redding, Sam and Dave, and Isaac Hayes screamed, shouted, begged, stomped, and cried, harkening back to the blues shouters of the Deep South. Atlantic's Jerry Wexler, who had participated in the earliest phase of soul music with his productions for Solomon Burke ("Just Out of Reach" [1961]), began recording Franklin as well as Wilson Pickett, one of soul's premier vocalists, in Fame Studios in Florence, Alabama, where the arrangements were largely spontaneous and surprisingly sparse-strong horn lines supported by a rhythm section focused on boiling funk.

Founded in Memphis in 1960 by country music fiddle player Jim Stewart and his sister Estelle Axton, following a previous false start with Satellite Records, Stax maintained a down-home, family atmosphere during its early years. Black and white musicians and singers worked together in relaxed conditions, where nobody looked at a clock or worried about union session rates, at the recording studio in a converted movie theatre at 926 East McLemore. They created records from ideas jotted down on bits of paper, phrases remembered from gospel songs, and rhythm licks that might make the kids on American Bandstand dance.

BOOKER T. AND THE MG'S

Organist Booker T. Jones (born November 12, 1944, Memphis, Tennessee, U.S.), drummer Al Jackson, Jr. (born November 27, 1935, Memphis—died October 1, 1975, Memphis), guitarist Steve Cropper (born Oct. 21, 1941, Willow Spring, Missouri), and bassist Donald ("Duck") Dunn (born November 24, 1941, Memphis—died May 13, 2012, Tokyo, Japan) had numerous hits as Booker T. and the MG's, and they made many more records as the rhythm section (and, in effect, producers) for most of the recordings at Stax during the decade, sometimes aided and abetted by pianist Isaac Hayes and lyricist David Porter, who teamed up as writer-producers in 1964.

With their signature tune, "Green Onions," and other enticing melodies such as "Boot-Leg" (1965), "Hip Hug-Her" (1967), and "Time Is Tight" (1969), Booker T. and the MG's (for "Memphis Group") brought the Memphis Sound to millions worldwide. When "Green Onions" became a million-selling hit in 1962, Jones was only 18. Already a veteran of the Memphis scene, he brought together Cropper (who practically resided at Stax Records), Jackson (who replaced Liam Steinberg), and Dunn. United by a passion for soul music, they became the core of a shifting alignment of musicians (including the Mar-Keys, the Bar-Kays, and the Memphis Horns) that acted as the house band for Stax Records, assisting in the creation of countless masterworks by such performers as Otis Redding and Sam and Dave. The group's racial composition—Jones and Jackson were black, and Cropper and Dunn were white—mirrored the hopes of the integrationist era. They played together until 1971 and re-formed periodically thereafter, though without the impact they had in the 1960s. Booker T. and the MG's were inducted into the Rock and Roll Hall of Fame in 1992.

Many Stax records featured a distinctive horn sound, and their bass-heavy bottom end had a powerful impact when played on jukeboxes and in dance clubs. Wexler was the earliest industry figure to recognize the potential of this Memphis Sound. He made a deal that allowed Atlantic to distribute Stax both nationally and internationally; he also was the catalyst for several milestone records made by singers from out of town: "Respect" (1965) by Otis Redding (from Georgia), whose records were released on the subsidiary label Volt; "In the Midnight Hour" (1965) by Wilson Pickett (from Alabama by way of Detroit), released on Atlantic; and "Soul Man (1962) by Sam and Dave (from Florida).

OTIS REDDING

One of the great soul stylists of the 1960s, Otis Redding (born September 9, 1941, Dawson, Georgia, U.S.—died December 10, 1967, near Madison, Wisconsin) was raised in Macon, Georgia, where he was deeply influenced by the subtle grace of Sam Cooke and the raw energy of Little Richard. In the late 1950s Redding joined Richard's band, the Upsetters, after Richard had gone solo. It was as a Little Richard imitator that Redding experienced his first minor hit, "Shout Bamalama," for the Confederate label of Athens, Georgia.

The story of Redding's breakthrough is part of soul music mythology. Redding joined Johnny Jenkins's Pinetoppers, a local Georgia band, and also served as the group's driver. When the group traveled to Memphis, Tennessee, to record at the famed Stax studios, Redding sang two songs of his own at the end of the session. One of the two, "These

Arms of Mine" (1962), launched his career, attracting both a record label executive (Jim Stewart) and a manager (Phil Walden) who passionately believed in his talent.

Redding's open-throated singing became the measure of the decade's great soul artists. Unabashedly emotional, he sang with overwhelming power and irresistible sincerity. "Otis wore his heart on his sleeve," said Jerry Wexler, who brought Redding to a national market.

The hits came fast and furiously— "I've Been Loving You Too Long (to Stop Now)" (1965), "Respect" (1965), "Satisfaction" (1966), "Fa-Fa-Fa-Fa-Fa (Sad Song)" (1966). Redding's influence extended beyond his gritty vocals. As a composer, especially with his frequent partner Steve Cropper, he introduced a new sort of rhythm-and-blues line—lean, clean, and steely strong. He arranged his songs as he wrote them, singing horn and rhythm parts to the musicians and, in general, sculpting his total sound. That sound, the Stax signature, would resonate for decades to come. Redding became a de facto leader presiding over a band that would prove as influential as the great rhythm-and-blues aggregations that preceded it, units associated with Ray Charles and James Brown.

The rapport between Redding and his rhythm section—Cropper on guitar, Donald ("Duck") Dunn on bass,

Al Jackson on drums, and Booker T. Jones on keyboards (known collectively as Booker T. and the MG's)—was extraordinary. Redding proved to be an adept duet partner as well; his hits with labelmate Carla Thomas ("Tramp" and "Knock on Wood," 1967) added to his romantic aura.

When the Stax/Volt Revue stormed Europe, Redding led the brigade. He converted hippiedom to soul music at the 1967 Monterey (California) Pop Festival and was just entering a new phase of popularity when tragedy struck. On December 10, 1967, a chartered plane crashed into a Wisconsin lake. Victims included Redding and his backing band. Redding was 26 years old.

Ironically, the across-the-board success Redding had sought was realized only after his death. His most haunting composition, cowritten with Cropper, shot to the top of the charts and became his only number one hit: "(Sittin' on) The Dock of the Bay" (1968), a bittersweet lament of indolence and love. The public mourned his passing by playing his records. During 1968 three other Redding songs—"The Happy Song (Dum Dum)," "Amen," and "Papa's Got a Brand New Bag"—hit the charts. He remains a giant of the genre, a much-revered master of straight-ahead soul singing. Redding was inducted into the Rock and Roll Hall of Fame in 1989.

SAM AND DAVE

Samuel Moore (born Oct. 12, 1935, Miami, Florida, U.S.) and David Prater (born May 9, 1937, Ocilla, Georgia—died April 9, 1988) were gospel group veterans when they joined forces in Miami in 1961. They recorded for Roulette Records before Jerry Wexler signed them and sent them to record for Stax/Volt Records. There, backed by Stax's extraordinary house band, Sam and Dave became the premier messengers for the Hayes-Porter team. Among their hits were "You Don't Know Like I Know" (1965), "Hold On! I'm a Comin'" (1966), and the ballad "When Something Is Wrong with My Baby" (1967). "Soul Man," their biggest hit, reached number two on the pop chart in 1967. Nicknamed "Double Dynamite" as a result of their exciting stage shows, Prater and Moore reputedly came to greatly dislike each other and seldom spoke. They broke up in 1970 but re-formed a number of times in the next 10 years. Prater was killed in a car crash in 1988, four years before Sam and Dave were inducted into the Rock and Roll Hall of Fame.

WILSON PICKETT

Singer-songwriter Wilson Pickett (born March 18, 1941, Prattville, Alabama, U.S.—died January 19, 2006, Reston, Virginia) was a product of the Southern black church, and gospel was at the core of his musical manner and onstage persona. He testified rather than sang, preached rather than crooned. His explosive delivery was marked by the fervour of religious conviction, no matter how secular the songs he sang.

Along with thousands of other Southern farmworkers, Pickett migrated in the 1950s to industrial Detroit, Michigan, where his father worked in an auto plant. His first recording experience was in pure gospel. He sang with the Violinaires and the Spiritual Five, modeling himself after Julius Cheeks of the Sensational Nightingales, a thunderous shouter.

Pickett's switch to secular music came quickly. As a member of the Falcons, a hardcore rhythm-and-blues vocal group, he sang lead on his own composition "I Found a Love" (1962), one of the songs that interested Jerry Wexler in Pickett as a solo artist. "Pickett was a pistol," said Wexler, who nicknamed him "the Wicked Pickett" and sent him to Memphis to write with Steve Cropper. The result was a smash single, "In the Midnight Hour" (1965). From that moment on, Pickett was a star. With his dazzling good looks and confident demeanour, he stood as a leading exponent of the Southern-fried school of soul singing. His unadorned straight-from-the-gut approach was accepted, even revered, by a civil-rights-minded pop culture.

After his initial string of smashes— "Land of 1000 Dances" (1966), "Mustang Sally" (1966), and "Funky Broadway" (1967)—Pickett was successfully produced by Philadelphians Kenny Gamble and Leon Huff, who took a bit of the edge off his fiery style on "Engine Number 9" (1970) and "Don't Let the Green Grass Fool You" (1971). Before leaving Atlantic, Pickett enjoyed another run of smashes, including "Don't Knock My Love" (1971), "Call My Name, I'll Be There" (1971), and "Fire and Water" (1972). The advent of funk bands and disco resulted in a decline in Pickett's popularity, although there are critics who consider "Groove City" (1979) on EMI, his one nod to disco, a dance groove of monumental stature. Although his output began to slow in the 1980s, Pickett continued to perform into the early 21st century, and his influence on younger generations of soulful singers, from Johnny Gill to Jonny Lang, remained strong. He was inducted into the Rock and Roll Hall of Fame in 1991.

Toward the end of the 1960s, the interracial harmony at Stax was disturbed by the social and political tension sweeping the nation, which culminated in the murder of Martin Luther King, Jr., in a nearby motel. Still under its original management but represented publicly by Al Bell, the black promotion man who became vice-president and co-owner,

MUSCLE SHOALS STUDIOS: "LAND OF 1000 DANCES"

Muscle Shoals, Alabama, was the last place anyone wanted to go to make a record: not only was it inconvenient (the absence of direct flights from New York City or Los Angeles meant changing planes in Atlanta, Georgia, or Memphis, Tennessee), it was dry (no bars). But the determination of one man and the musicianship of several others drew customers from near and far and kept the three adjacent towns of Muscle Shoals, Florence, and Sheffield on the musical map for 40 years. Percy Sledge launched his career with "When a Man Loves a Woman" (recorded at Quinn Ivy's studio in Sheffield), and Joe Tex, Wilson Pickett, Aretha Franklin, and the Staple Singers were among the many artists who recorded the first Top Ten hits of their careers in Muscle Shoals after years of trying elsewhere.

Songwriter-engineer-turned-producer Rick Hall set up Fame Studios in Florence in 1961. He recruited his session musicians from a local group—Dan Penn and the Pallbearers—who played on the studio's first hit, Arthur Alexander's "You Better Move On." Atlanta-based publisher Lowery Music provided regular work, and, after Jerry Wexler brought Pickett to Muscle Shoals to record "Land of 1000 Dances" in 1966, out-of-state visitors became more frequent. When the first group of session musicians moved on (first to Nashville, Tennessee, later to play with Bob Dylan, Neil Young, and others), Hall pulled together a magnificent replacement team, including Spooner Oldham on keyboards, Jimmy Johnson on guitars, David Hood on bass, and Roger Hawkins on drums. Most of this group played on Franklin's breakthrough single, "I Never Loved a Man (the Way I Love You)," and then left Fame to set up their own Muscle Shoals Sound Studio nearby. In contrast to the racially diverse session players of Memphis, these musicians were all white. But, steeped in gospel and rhythm and blues, they contributed to some of the most soulful records of the era.

Other artists and producers followed Wexler's lead. Etta James, with her earthshaking delivery and take-no-prisoners approach, traveled to Muscle Shoals to record "Tell Mama" (1967), one of the decade's enduring soul anthems, written by singer and songwriter Clarence Carter. Percy Sledge's supersmooth "When a Man Loves a Woman" (1966), recorded in Sheffield, became the first Southern soul song to reach number one on the pop charts.

Stax achieved its greatest commercial success during the early 1970s with hits recorded in Detroit, Chicago, and Muscle Shoals, Alabama, as well as in its own studios, by Johnnie Taylor, Hayes, the Staple Singers, the Dramatics, and others. Many of the songs of this era, along with members of the original rhythm section, resurfaced in the movie *The Blues Brothers* (1980).

OTHER VOICES, OTHER PLACES

By the decade's end even Motown, the most conservative of the soul labels, had begun to release issue-oriented records, especially with Norman Whitfield's dynamic productions for the Temptations ("Cloud Nine" [1968]) and Edwin Starr ("War"). But soul was not restricted to the South and Detroit.

SOLOMON BURKE

Solomon Burke (born March 21, 1940, Philadelphia, Pennsylvania, U.S.—died October 10, 2010, Haarlemmermeer, Netherlands) helped to usher in the soul music era in the early 1960s by merging rhythm and blues with the gospel style he learned in the church that his family established in Philadelphia. Burke was both a preacher and the host of a gospel radio program by age 12. He began recording in 1955 but did not have his first national hit until 1961, with a rhythm-and-blues version of a country ballad, "Just Out of Reach." His recordings, most of which were produced in New York City, incorporated gospel-derived vocal techniques—shouted interjections, an exhortatory recitation, melisma, and rasping timbre. At Atlantic Records, under producer Bert Berns, Burke became one of the first rhythm-and-blues performers to be called a soul artist, based on his success with "Cry to Me" (1962), "If You Need Me" (1963), "Goodbye Baby (Baby Goodbye)" (1964), "Got to Get You off My Mind" (1965), and his last Top 40 pop hit, "Tonight's the Night" (1965).

After the mid-1960s Burke continued to record but with lessening success, last placing a record on the rhythm-and-blues chart in 1978. He remained a popular performer on the blues festival and club circuit into the early 21st century. He was traveling to the Netherlands for a performance in October 2010 when he died at Schiphol airport near Amsterdam. Burke was inducted into the Rock and Roll Hall of Fame in 2001.

"IT'S ALL RIGHT": CHICAGO SOUL

Several black music producers—including Roquel ("Billy") Davis and Carl Davis (who were not related), Johnny Pate (who also was an arranger), and Curtis Mayfield—developed a recognizable Chicago sound that flourished from the late 1950s to the mid-1970s. This lightly gospelized rhythm and blues, which came to be known as Chicago soul, replaced the raucous blues of South Side bars with sophisticated, jazzy arrangements confected in recording studios and featuring melodic vocals backed by brass sections and strings.

The first record from the city with a distinctly soulful sound was Jerry Butler and the Impressions' "For Your Precious Love" (1958). Butler and the Impressions (Curtis Mayfield, Sam Gooden, and brothers Richard and Arthur Brooks) parted company to pursue parallel careers but remained in contact, and the group's guitarist, Mayfield, provided Butler's next big hit, "He Will Break Your Heart" (1960); its gospel structure established the blueprint for the sound of the city for the next 10 years.

Butler left in 1958 and was replaced by Fred Cash; the Brooks brothers left in 1962. With the group reduced to a trio, Mayfield (born June 3, 1942, Chicago, Illinois, U.S.—died December 26, 1999, Roswell, Georgia), along with Gooden and Cash, devised a much-imitated vocal style, a pronounced three-part alternating lead, which allowed Mayfield's delicate high tenor to be balanced by Gooden's bass and Cash's low tenor. Derived from gospel music, this switch-off technique called for each vocalist to take a turn with the lead part while the others provided backing harmony. It was later adopted by groups such as Sly and the Family Stone and Earth, Wind and Fire.

A remarkably innovative guitarist, the self-taught Mayfield tuned his instrument to a natural chord to achieve a subtle, lyrical sound. Many other guitarists in Chicago imitated his playing, and the Mayfield style showed up on innumerable soul records made in his hometown. Beginning with his earliest songs—such as "Gypsy Woman" (1961), "It's All Right" (1963), "Keep On Pushing" (1964), and "People Get Ready" (1965)—when he was lead vocalist of the Impressions, Mayfield wrote highly inspirational, humanistic pieces concerned with African American uplift. He also was a major contributor of songs to other soul performers—most of them from Chicago. Among those who recorded his compositions were Jan Bradley, Jerry Butler, Gene Chandler, Aretha Franklin, Walter Jackson, Gladys Knight and the Pips, Major Lance, and the Staple Singers. In the late 1960s, with such songs as "We're a Winner" (1967) and "Choice of Colors" (1969), recorded with the Impressions, Mayfield played a crucial role in transforming black popular music into a voice for social concern during the struggle for civil rights.

In 1961 he became one of the first African Americans to found his own music publishing company. Six years later he established the highly successful Curtom Records, which became a leading producer of soundtrack albums for black-oriented films and for which Mayfield and such artists as Gene Chandler, Major Lance, and the Five Stairsteps recorded. Mayfield left the Impressions in 1970 to work as a soloist and subsequently became a major force in the development of funk, with such songs as "(Don't Worry) If There's a Hell Below We're All Going to Go," "Beautiful Brother of Mine," and "We People Who Are Darker Than Blue." Although he achieved considerable recognition for such albums as *Curtis* (1970) and *Curtis/Live!* (1971), it was through the recording of soundtracks for motion pictures that Mayfield achieved his biggest success, particularly with *Superfly* (1972). Mayfield's last Top Ten rhythm-and-blues hit was "Only You Babe" in 1976. He was paralyzed from the neck down by a freak accident during a concert in 1990. He was inducted into the Rock and Roll Hall of Fame as a member of the Impressions in 1991 and as a solo artist in 1999.

Billy Davis had been Berry Gordy, Jr.,'s songwriting partner before joining the artists-and-repertoire (A&R) staff at Chess, where he worked with most of the label's roster, including Etta James and Sugar Pie DeSanto. Following the success of Gene Chandler's "Duke of Earl" (1961), producer Carl Davis was appointed head of A&R for OKeh Records, where he recruited Mayfield to write for several artists including Lance. Davis then moved to Brunswick Records, where he produced one of Jackie Wilson's finest records, "(Your Love Keeps Lifting Me) Higher and Higher" (1967). He subsequently set up his own Dakar label, whose singles by Tyrone Davis—"Can I Change My Mind?" (1969) and "Turn Back the Hands of Time" (1970)—were classics of wistful regret.

THE STAPLE SINGERS

Any barriers between the sacred and the sensual that Aretha Franklin may have left standing were blown away by Mavis Staples (born 1940, Chicago, Illinois, U.S.) and her thrilling contralto. Begun by Mavis's guitarist father, Roebuck ("Pops") Staples (born December 2, 1915, Winona, Mississippi—died December 19, 2000, Dolton, Illinois) in the early 1950s, the Staple Singers included Mavis's sisters Cleotha (born 1934,

The Staple Singers. From left to right: Mavis Staples, Cleotha Staples, Pervis Staples, and Roebuck Staples. Michael Ochs Archives/Getty Images

Mississippi) and Yvonne (born 1939, Chicago), who joined after the group had been performing for a while, and her brother Pervis (born 1939, Chicago), who left in the early 1970s. As a teenager Roebuck had picked cotton at Dockery's plantation, where he was influenced by legendary guitarist Charley Patton and other seminal blues musicians, and he moved to Chicago in the mid-1930s. By the mid-1950s his terse lead guitar and the family's otherworldly harmonies had made the Staples a leading gospel group. They recorded memorable versions of "Uncloudy Day" (1959) and other sacred classics for the Vee Jay label.

The Staples finally succeeded in breaking into the secular market after the group signed with Stax Records in 1968 and made a series of records marked by the seamless blending of genres and an infectious optimism. "Heavy Makes You Happy" (1971) was their first secular hit, and "Respect Yourself" (1971) paved the way for "I'll Take You There" (1972), a number one single on both the pop and rhythm-and-blues charts. The group had a modest hit with a cover of Talking Heads' "Slippery People" in 1984, and Roebuck had a small role in *True Stories* (1986), a film by Talking Heads frontman David Byrne. While the Staples remained active into the 1990s, the solo efforts of its individual members began to take precedence. Roebuck's solo album *Father Father* (1994) won a Grammy Award for best contemporary blues album. Mavis, who had maintained a simultaneous solo career beginning in the late 1960s, found renewed success in the 21st century. In 2004 she released *Have a Little Faith*, a Delta blues-flavoured collection of soul, as a tribute to her father, whose influence—musical, parental, and spiritual—was everywhere evident on the album. She followed up with *We'll Never Turn Back* in 2007, and in 2010 she released *You Are Not Alone*, a collection of gospel standards and new songs produced by Wilco frontman Jeff Tweedy that was awarded the Grammy Award for best Americana album. The Staple Singers were inducted into the Rock and Roll Hall of Fame in 1999, and in 2005 the group was awarded a Grammy for lifetime achievement.

HI RECORDS AND AL GREEN

Soul also flowered in New Orleans, Louisiana, in the ultra-funky work of Art Neville's group the Meters. In the 1970s Atlantic Records produced smoldering soul smashes in New York City—notably by Aretha Franklin and Donny Hathaway; and Stevie Wonder and the Jackson 5 created some of the era's great soul records in Los Angeles. Back in Memphis in the early 1970s the chain of racially mixed musics made by integrated musicians—from the output of Sun Records to that of Stax/Volt and Chips Moman's American Sound Studios—was broken, largely as a consequence of urban blight and the coalition-splintering shock of the King assassination. In the aftermath, however, Willie Mitchell created a new soul style with vocalist Al Green at Hi Records. Hi had been around since the late 1950s, with instrumental hits by Elvis Presley's former bassist, Bill Black, and by Mitchell, a former jazz bandleader who took over as artists-and-repertoire man.

Hi's Royal Recording Studios, at 1320 South Lauderdale Street, just off Highway 61 in a predominantly African American portion of the city, were, like Stax's, located in a former movie theatre. Mitchell used the unusual acoustics caused partly by the theatre's sloping floor to construct a new sound. He slowed soul's tempo and emphasized a percussive ¼ beat, utilizing the talents of drummer Al Jackson (formerly of Booker T. and the MG's) and the Hodges brothers—Leroy (bass), Charles (keyboards), and Teenie (guitar). The first hint of the new sound was Ann Peebles's "Part Time Love" (1970), but its full glory was revealed in a sublime series of hits by Al Green (remembered for his trademark white suit) from 1971 to 1975. These sexy songs for adults were the cornerstone of some of soul's most luxuriant music. By further transforming the essential relationship in soul music between the sacred and the secular, Green (born April 13, 1946, Forrest City, Arkansas, U.S.) followed the musical and spiritual path of his greatest inspiration, Sam Cooke. At the height of Green's commercial success, however, he sacrificed his fame in order to fully dedicate himself to his religious faith.

In 1964, after his family moved from Arkansas to Michigan, Green and some friends formed the Creations and toured the chitlin circuit (venues that catered to African American audiences) in the South before renaming themselves Al Green and the Soul Mates three years later. They formed their own record label, releasing the single "Back Up Train," which enjoyed moderate success on the rhythm-and-blues charts in 1968. The watershed moment for Green came in Texas in 1968 when he met Mitchell. Obscurity was threatening to end Green's fledgling career, but with Mitchell's help he became a star in short order. After releasing a cover version of the Beatles' "I Want to Hold Your Hand" in 1969, which exhibited his awe-inspiring vocal agility, Green recorded a fine remake of the Temptations' "I Can't Get Next to You," and it reached number one on the soul charts in 1971. But it was "Tired of Being Alone" (1971), written

Al Green playing a guitar. GAB Archive/Redferns/Getty Images

by Green, that suggested his extraordinary potential. It sold more than a million copies, preparing the way for "Let's Stay Together," the title track from Green's first gold album.

"Let's Stay Together" was his biggest hit, reaching number one on both the rhythm-and-blues and pop charts in 1972. Written by Green, Mitchell, and Al Jackson, the song reflected Mitchell's musical vision. In comparison with the grittier sound of Memphis neighbour Stax/Volt, Green's recordings with Mitchell offered a sophisticated and softened melody cradled by a distinctive bass sound. Green delivered gospel intensity, effortlessly soaring to the highest falsetto or plunging into a husky groan cloaked in hushed sensuality. From the tender "I'm Still in Love with You" (1972) and "Call Me (Come Back Home)" (1973) to the earthy "Love and Happiness" (1973) and "Here I Am (Come and Take Me)" (1973), Green and Mitchell experienced a string of hits through the early 1970s.

In the mid-1970s Green became a minister, establishing his own church. By 1980 he had devoted himself completely to his ministry and to gospel music. Later in that decade he cautiously reemerged from his spiritual seclusion and resumed performances of his most celebrated works alongside his popular gospel recordings. After a commercially disappointing comeback effort in 1995, Green came close to recapturing his trademark 1970s sound on *I Can't Stop* (2003), which he followed with *Everything's OK* (2005). Green won a new generation of fans with *Lay It Down* (2008), featuring guest vocals by neo-soul artists John Legend, Anthony Hamilton, and Corinne Bailey Rae; the album earned him a

pair of Grammy Awards. Green was inducted into the Rock and Roll Hall of Fame in 1995.

THE SOUND OF PHILADELPHIA

The Sound of Philadelphia in the 1970s was the bridge between Memphis soul, international disco, Detroit pop, and Hi-NRG (high energy; the ultrafast dance music popular primarily in gay clubs in the 1980s). African American-run Philadelphia International Records was the vital label of the era; its sound was a timely mix of swishing high-hat cymbals and social awareness, of growling soul vocals and sweeping strings. The founding fathers were Philadelphian Kenny Gamble and New Jersey-born Leon Huff, writer-producers who had made their way through the collapsing Philadelphia music industry of the 1960s. They were reinforced by singer-turned-writer Linda Creed and writer-arranger Thom Bell, who had helped create the sound of the Delfonics at the city's other main label, Philly Groove. Together they created a new kind of pop soul, which can appear clichéd when dissected but was immensely popular on the dance floor. Based on the rhythmic talents of the Sigma Studios session men, who had a hit of their own as MFSB, Philadelphia International music featured unusual instrumentation—French horns, for example—and adult sensibilities delivered by adult vocalists.

After nearly 20 years in the business, Harold Melvin and the Bluenotes became stars, and lead vocalist Teddy Pendergrass became an archetypal 1970s sex symbol. Beginning as a gospel singer in Philadelphia churches, Pendergrass (born Theodore DeReese Pendergrass, March 26, 1950, Kingstree, South Carolina, U.S.—died January 13, 2010, Bryn Mawr, Pennsylvania) taught himself to play drums and joined the Blue Notes in 1969. The group's 1972 eponymous debut album for Philadelphia International produced the singles "I Miss You" and Grammy-nominated "If You Don't Know Me by Now," and Pendergrass joined the ranks of R&B's elite male vocalists. While he lacked the vocal range of Al Green or the musical virtuosity of Stevie Wonder, Pendergrass brought an unbridled masculinity to his stage presence. Embarking on a solo career in 1976, Pendergrass capitalized on his baritone lothario image, most notably with his trademark "ladies only" concerts. He scored hits with the singles "I Don't Love You Anymore" and "Love T.K.O."

After an automobile accident in 1982 left him paralyzed from the waist down, his recording future appeared to be in doubt. But after a year of rehabilitation, he released a new album that ultimately went gold.

He returned to the stage in 1985, performing in his wheelchair at the Live Aid benefit concert in Philadelphia.

"Me and Mrs. Jones" (1972), a tale of implied infidelity, launched nightclub balladeer Billy Paul. The O'Jays, also veterans with a 10-year recording history behind them, reached the Top Ten with "Back Stabbers" (1972) and "Love Train" (1973), both social commentaries in a successfully naive vein. Where Gamble and Huff led, disco followed—the Ritchie Family's "Best Disco in Town" (1976) was recorded at Sigma, as was the Village People's "YMCA" (1978). Philadelphia's final big hit, the anthemic "Ain't No Stoppin' Us Now" (1979) by (Gene) McFadden and (John) Whitehead, came as dance music underwent one of its episodic black-white schisms. A couple of years later, Daryl Hall and John Oates—the favourite white sons of Philadelphia soul—grafted their traditional rhythm-and-blues voicings onto the new black rhythms of hip-hop.

BLUE-EYED SOUL

In contrast to the scores of white performers who simply covered—some would say stole—the compositions of black artists, the practitioners of blue-eyed soul devoted themselves to and identified with contemporary black music in a manner rare outside the jazz community. The premier blue-eyed soul performers of the 1960s were the Righteous Brothers, comprising Bill Medley (born September 19, 1940, Los Angeles, California, U.S.) and Bobby Hatfield (born August 10, 1940, Beaver Dam, Wisconsin—died November 5, 2003, Kalamazoo, Michigan), and the Rascals (known for a time as the Young Rascals), whose principal members were Felix Cavaliere (born November 29, 1943, Pelham, New York), Gene Cornish (born May 14, 1946, Ottawa, Ontario, Canada), Eddie Brigati (born October 22, 1946, New York, New York), and Dino Danelli (born July 23, 1945, New York). Produced by Phil Spector, "You've Lost That Lovin' Feelin'" (1964) and "Unchained Melody" (1965) earned the Righteous Brothers considerable commercial success. The Rascals' hits "Good Lovin'" (1966) and "Groovin'" (1967) demonstrated promising originality rather than mere imitation.

Hits like the Soul Survivors' "Expressway to Your Heart" (1967) and "I've Been Hurt" (1969) by Bill Deal and the Rhondels emerged from a field of white soul performers that included Bob Kuban and the In-Men, from St. Louis; the Box Tops (featuring future Big Star frontman Alex Chilton), from Memphis; and Mitch Ryder and the Detroit Wheels, from Detroit.

Soul became a permanent part of the grammar of American popular culture. Its underlying virtues—direct emotional delivery, ethnic pride, and respect for its own artistic sources—live on as dynamic and dramatic influences on musicians throughout the world. To varying degrees, the power and personality of the form were absorbed in disco, funk, and hip-hop, styles that owe their existence to soul.

CHAPTER 11

Psychedelia, San Francisco, and the Rock Paradox

On both the East and West coasts, bohemia had taken an interest in youth music again. In San Francisco, for example, folk and blues musicians, artists, and poets came together in loose collectives (most prominently the Grateful Dead and the Jefferson Airplane) to make acid rock as an unfolding psychedelic experience, and rock became the musical soundtrack for a new youth culture, the hippies.

The hippie movement of the late 1960s in the United States fed back into the British rock scene. British beat groups also defined their music as art, not commerce, and felt themselves to be constrained by technology rather than markets. The Beatles made the move from pop to rock on their 1967 album, *Sgt. Pepper's Lonely Hearts Club Band*, symbolically identifying with the new hippie era, while bands such as Pink Floyd and Cream set new standards of musical skill and technical imagination. This was the setting in which Jimi Hendrix became the rock musician's rock musician. He was a model not just in his virtuosity and inventiveness as a musician but also in his stardom and his commercial charisma.

By the end of the 1960s the great paradox of rock had become apparent: rock musicians' commitment to artistic integrity—their disdain for chart popularity—was bringing them unprecedented wealth. Sales of rock albums and concert tickets reached levels never before seen in popular music. And, as the new musical ideology was being articulated in magazines such as *Rolling Stone*, so it was being commercially packaged by emergent record companies such as Warner Brothers in the United States and Island in Britain. Rock fed both off and into hippie rebellion (as celebrated by the Woodstock festival of 1969), and it fed both off and into a buoyant new music business (also celebrated by Woodstock). This music and audience were now where the money lay; the Woodstock musicians seemed to have tapped into an insatiable demand, whether for "progressive" rock and formal experiment, heavy metal and a bass-driven blast of high-volume blues, or singer-songwriters and sensitive self-exploration.

HEAD SOUNDS: PSYCHEDELIC ROCK

In 1967 the Beatles were in Abbey Road Studios putting the finishing touches on their album *Sgt. Pepper's Lonely Hearts Club Band*. At one point Paul McCartney wandered

The multi-hued bus, nicknamed "Further," belonging to Ken Kesey and the Merry Pranksters, parked at the Woodstock Music and Art Fair in 1969. John Dominis/Time & Life Pictures/Getty Images

down the corridor and heard what was then a new young band called Pink Floyd working on their hypnotic debut, *The Piper at the Gates of Dawn*. He listened for a moment, then came rushing back. "Hey guys," he reputedly said, "There's a new band in there and they're gonna steal our thunder."

With their mix of blues, music hall influences, Lewis Carroll references, and dissonant experimentation, Pink Floyd was one of the key bands of the 1960s psychedelic revolution, a pop culture movement that emerged with American and British rock, before sweeping through film, literature, and the visual arts. The music was largely inspired by hallucinogens, or so-called "mind-expanding" drugs such as marijuana and LSD (lysergic acid diethylamide; "acid"), and attempted to re-create drug-induced states through the use of overdriven guitar, amplified feedback, and droning guitar motifs influenced by Eastern music.

This psychedelic consciousness was seeded, in the United States, by countercultural gurus such as Dr. Timothy Leary, a Harvard University professor who began researching LSD as a tool of self-discovery from 1960, and writer Ken Kesey. At a Veterans Administration hospital in Menlo Park, California, Kesey was a paid volunteer experimental subject, taking mind-altering drugs and reporting on their effects. This experience and his work as an aide at the hospital served as background for his best-known novel, *One Flew Over the Cuckoo's Nest* (1962; film 1975), which is set in a mental hospital. Later, in and around San Francisco, Kesey and his Merry Pranksters staged Acid Tests—multimedia "happenings" set to the music of the Warlocks (later the Grateful Dead) and documented by cultural historian and novelist Tom Wolfe in the literary classic *The Electric Kool-Aid Acid Test* (1968)—and traversed the country during the mid-1960s on a kaleidoscope-colored school bus.

TIMOTHY LEARY

The son of a U.S. Army officer, Timothy Leary (born October 22, 1920, Springfield, Massachusetts, U.S.—died May 31, 1996, Beverly Hills, California) was raised in a Roman Catholic household and attended Holy Cross College, the U.S. Military Academy at West Point, and the University of Alabama (B.A., 1943). In 1950 he received a doctorate in psychology from the University of California, Berkeley, where he was an assistant professor until 1955. During the 1950s Leary developed an egalitarian model for interaction between the psychotherapist and the patient, promoted new techniques of group therapy, and published a

LSD AND HALLUCINOGENS

Hallucinogens are substances that produce psychological effects that are normally associated only with dreams, schizophrenia, or religious exaltation. They produce changes in perception, thought, and feeling, ranging from distortions of what is sensed (illusions) to sensing objects where none exist (hallucinations). Hallucinogens heighten sensory signals, but this is often accompanied by loss of control over what is experienced.

The psychopharmacological drugs that have aroused widespread interest and bitter controversy are those that produce marked aberrations in behaviour or perception. Among the most prevalent of these are d-lysergic acid diethylamide, or LSD-25, which originally was derived from ergot (*Claviceps purpurea*), a fungus on rye and wheat; mescaline, the active principle of the peyote cactus (*Lophophora williamsii*), which grows in the southwestern United States and Mexico; and psilocybin and psilocin, which come from certain mushrooms (notably two Mexican species, *Psilocybe mexicana* and *Stropharia cubensis*). Other hallucinogens include bufotenine, originally isolated from the skin of toads; harmine, from the seed coats of a plant of the Middle East and Mediterranean region; and the synthetic compounds methylenedioxyamphetamine (MDA), methylenedioxymethamphetamine (MDMA), and phencyclidine (PCP). Tetrahydrocannabinol (THC), the active ingredient in cannabis, or marijuana, obtained from the leaves and tops of plants in the genus *Cannabis*, is also sometimes classified as a hallucinogen.

In the 1960s LSD was proposed for use in the treatment of neuroses, especially for patients who were recalcitrant to more conventional psychotherapeutic procedures. LSD also was tried as a treatment for alcoholism and to reduce the suffering of terminally ill cancer patients. It was studied as an adjunct in the treatment of narcotic addiction, of children with autism, and of the so-called psychopathic personality. None of these uses were successful by the early 1990s, and most researchers concluded that there was no clinical value in the use of LSD.

The manufacture, possession, sale, transfer, and use of LSD came under the restrictions of the Drug Abuse Control Amendment of 1965. The following year the only authorized manufacturer of LSD in the United States withdrew the drug from the market and transferred its supplies to the federal government. Research projects have continued under the supervision of the National Institute of Mental Health, a governmental agency.

A critical player in the convergence of LSD and the hippie movement was Augustus Owsley Stanley III, a California-based underground chemist who manufactured several million doses of the drug. Owsley's efforts supplied the drug to several figures who would become advocates for LSD, including both Kesey and Leary (Owsley also was a personal supplier of LSD to the Grateful Dead). During the mid-1960s, LSD spread widely in the emerging counter-culture, and the shapes and colours characteristic of LSD-induced trips appear frequently in the visual art of the period. The drug also powerfully shaped the popular music of the 1960s and encouraged the mystical experimentation of these years.

system for classifying interpersonal behaviour. He acquired a reputation as a promising young scholar and was appointed to the position of lecturer at Harvard University in 1959.

At Harvard, Leary began experimenting with psilocybin, a synthesized form of the hallucinogenic agent found in certain mushrooms.

He concluded that psychedelic drugs could be effective in transforming personality and expanding human consciousness. Along with a colleague, he formed the Harvard Psychedelic Drug Research Program and began administering psilocybin to graduate students; he also shared the drug with several prominent artists, writers, and musicians. Leary explored the cultural and philosophical implications of psychedelic drugs; in contrast to those within the psychedelic research community who argued that the drugs should be used only by a small elite, Leary came to believe that the experience should be introduced to the general public, particularly to young people.

Leary's experiments were highly controversial, and he was dismissed from Harvard in 1963 after colleagues protested. During the mid-1960s Leary lived in a mansion in Millbrook, New York, where he formed the centre of a small hedonistic community and began to intensively explore LSD, a more powerful psychedelic drug. His research, which initially had emphasized careful control over the "set and setting" of the psychedelic experience, became increasingly undisciplined and unstructured. He traveled widely and gave many public lectures, especially on college campuses, and because of his high public profile, he became a focus of the emerging public debate over LSD. His phrase "turn on, tune in, drop out" became a popular counterculture slogan. Cultural conservatives saw Leary as a corrosive influence on society—Pres. Richard Nixon called him "the most dangerous man in America"—while many researchers felt that Leary delegitimized the serious study of psychedelic drugs.

After arrests in 1965 and 1968 for possession of marijuana and a prolonged legal battle, Leary was incarcerated in 1970. He soon escaped and became a fugitive, living outside the United States for more than two years until being recaptured in Afghanistan. He was freed in 1976 and settled in southern California.

THE GRATEFUL DEAD

Many psychedelic bands explored an LSD-influenced sense of abandonment in their music, moving away from standard rock rhythms and instrumentation. The Grateful Dead, for instance, created an improvisatory mix of country rock, blues, and acid R&B. Settling on their name in late 1965, the Grateful Dead coalesced from jug bands and musicians in the San Francisco area in the early 1960s. As the Warlocks, they had performed at Ken Kesey's Acid Test sound-and-light celebrations of the psychedelic experience. Remarkably eclectic—their backgrounds ranging from electronic experiments and jazz to bluegrass and folk—the Dead provided a key part of the free live music filling San Francisco during 1967's Summer of Love, when the city became a magnet for hippie baby boomers.

The original members were lead guitarist and vocalist Jerry Garcia (born August 1, 1942, San Francisco,

California, U.S.—died August 9, 1995, Forest Knolls, California), guitarist and vocalist Bob Weir (born October 16, 1947, San Francisco), keyboard player Ron ("Pigpen") McKernan (born September 8, 1945, San Bruno, California—died March 8, 1973, San Francisco), bassist Phil Lesh (born March 15, 1940, Berkeley, California), and drummer Bill Kreutzmann (born May 7, 1946, Palo Alto, California). Later members included drummer Mickey Hart (born September 1943, Long Island, New York), keyboard player Tom Constanten (born March 19, 1944, Longbranch, New Jersey), keyboard player Keith Godchaux (born July 19, 1948, San Francisco—died July 21, 1980, Marin County, California), vocalist Donna Godchaux (born August 22, 1947, San Francisco), and keyboard player and vocalist Brent Mydland (born October 21, 1952, Munich, West Germany [now Germany]—died July 26, 1990, Lafayette, California).

Even before they recorded their first album, the Dead were building an underground network of diehard fans. By the late 1960s the fans were legion and followed the band on the road. The Deadheads, as they were known, were the epitome of the counterculture. Draped in flowing scarves and granny dresses, they danced arrhythmically while the band onstage jammed for hours and hours. Thanks to them, the Dead eventually triumphed over standard music business wisdom, which assumed that an act had to have hit records to be a popular concert attraction. The unparalleled loyalty of the Deadheads made the band millionaires and endured until the Dead split up following the 1995 death of the group's leader, Jerry Garcia.

Although their studio sessions ranged from the amphetamine blues of *The Grateful Dead* (1967) to the jaggedly exploratory *Aoxomoxoa* (1969) to the lilting folk of *American Beauty* (1970), the Dead's strengths—and weaknesses—came most to the fore onstage. Their most artistically successful albums, *Live/Dead* (1969) and *Grateful Dead Live* (1971), were live recordings. A popular bumper sticker read, "There is nothing like a Grateful Dead concert." For better or worse, that was true. Pooling their eclectic talents, the Dead pioneered an energizing blend of rock instrumentation and jazzy improvisation; thanks to their laissez-faire and often drug-fueled stage attitudes, they often fell apart.

Few bands of any genre, however, could match the Dead at their best—fluid, open-eared interchanges, ecstatic mood swings, visceral impact. The Dead created a new form of American music. Like Jimi Hendrix, though they had imitators, they remained sui generis. The Grateful Dead were inducted into the

Rock and Roll Hall of Fame in 1994. While the Grateful Dead had ceased to exist following the death of Garcia, the remaining band members continued their "long, strange trip" with various interruptions. Weir, Lesh, Kreutzmann, and Hart formed the Other Ones and later dubbed themselves The Dead (dropping "Grateful" out of respect for Garcia).

THE JEFFERSON AIRPLANE

The Jefferson Airplane gained a huge following with its biting political lyrics, soaring harmonies, and hallucinogenic titles such as *Surrealistic Pillow* and "White Rabbit." The Jefferson Airplane was an important standard-bearer for the counterculture in the 1960s, but in its later incarnations it had hits with more mainstream material in the 1970s and '80s. The original members were Marty Balin (born Martyn Jerel Buchwald, January 30, 1943, Cincinnati, Ohio), Paul Kantner (born March 17, 1941, San Francisco, California), Jorma Kaukonen (born December 23, 1940, Washington, D.C.), Signe Anderson (born September 15, 1941, Seattle, Washington), Skip Spence (born April 18, 1946, Ontario, Canada—died 16, 1999, Santa Cruz, California), Jack Casady (born April 13, 1944, Washington, D.C.), and Bob Harvey. Later members included Grace Slick (born Grace Barnett Wing, October 30, 1939, Chicago, Illinois), Spencer Dryden (born April 7, 1938, New York, New York—died January 10, 2005, Penngrove, California), Papa John Creach (born May 28, 1917, Beaver Falls, Pennsylvania—died February 22, 1994, Los Angeles, California), David Freiberg (born August 24, 1938, Boston, Massachusetts), Craig Chaquico (born September 26, 1954, Sacramento, California), and Aynsley Dunbar (born January 10, 1946, Liverpool, Merseyside, England).

The band was started in the mid-1960s by former folk musicians; in late 1966, however, edgy-voiced ex-model Slick and the harder, rumbling rhythms pouring from bassist Casady and drummer Dryden transformed the Jefferson Airplane into a dance band with a social conscience. The Airplane was the first San Francisco-based band to land a major label contract. Their second album, *Surrealistic Pillow* (1967), produced two Top Ten singles, "White Rabbit" and "Somebody to Love," both cowritten by Slick for her previous band, the Great Society, and drew hordes of fans to San Francisco's Summer of Love pageantry. The city's Haight-Ashbury neighbourhood had become the centre of the burgeoning hippie counterculture, but the commercialism and crime that rapidly overtook that bohemian enclave in the love fest's wake were reflected in the bittersweet brilliance of the

Airplane's fourth album, *Crown of Creation* (1968).

Playing live at venues such as the Fillmore Auditorium, the band developed its crowd-pleasing version of the improvisational jamming that became the hallmark of the San Francisco sound pioneered by the Grateful Dead, Big Brother and the Holding Company (featuring Janis Joplin), and Santana, among others. Casady, Dryden, and guitarist Kaukonen slashed and soared through extended psychedelic blues while songwriters Kantner, Slick, and Balin did not so much harmonize on as cohabit melodies and lyrics. The best onstage document of their approach, *Bless Its Pointed Little Head*, was one of two album releases in 1969; the other, *Volunteers*, was a call for youth revolt, a reaction to the police riots of the 1968 Democratic National Convention in Chicago. In addition to its agitprop title song, the album included the postapocalyptic "Wooden Ships," cowritten by Kantner, David Crosby, and Stephen Stills. Volunteers was the Airplane's final creative peak.

The band, its membership constantly shifting, released albums for 20 years as the Jefferson Airplane, Jefferson Starship, and Starship. Although it experienced commercial success—most notably with 1975's chart-topping *Red Octopus* and its Top Ten single "Miracles"—the band never recaptured the moment when its music stood for something more, when the Airplane spoke for change on behalf of the culture that produced it. The Jefferson Airplane was inducted into the Rock and Roll Hall of Fame in 1996.

LOVE

In Los Angeles the Byrds created a jangly psychedelic folk augmented by rich vocal harmonies and orchestration with such hits as "Eight Miles High" and their cover of Bob Dylan's "Mr. Tambourine Man." Also in Los Angeles, the multiracial band Love played whimsical, free-flowing rock, fueled by the unique vision of their troubled frontman Arthur Lee. In addition to Lee (born 1945, Memphis, Tennessee, U.S.—died August 3, 2006, Memphis), the original members were Bryan MacLean (born 1947, Los Angeles, California—died December 25, 1998), John Echols (born 1945, Memphis), Ken Forssi (born 1943, Cleveland, Ohio—died February 10, 1998), Don Conka, and Alban ("Snoopy") Pfisterer (born 1947, Switzerland). Later members included Jay Donnellan, Frank Fayad, George Suranovitch, and Tjay Cantrelli.

At the centre of the band was Lee, an enigmatic personality, soulful vocalist, and highly creative, if sometimes surreal, songwriter. He absorbed and transformed garage and Byrds-influenced folk-rock styles on the band's first three albums, incorporating jazz, blues, and psychedelic influences. Each of those albums generated a charting single, but the band's otherwise moderate sales little indicate Love's impact. Following the lush third album, *Forever Changes* (1968), a folk-rock masterpiece, the band fragmented. Lee continued Love into the 1970s with new musicians, tending toward a heavier sound influenced by his friend Jimi Hendrix. An international cult of loyal fans supported Lee's later resurfacings in the 1980s and '90s. In 1996 Lee received a 12-year prison sentence for illegal gun possession. Released in 2001, he resumed touring with Love the following year.

THE DOORS

The Doors was the creative vehicle for singer Jim Morrison, one of rock music's mythic figures. The members were Morrison (born James Douglas Morrison, December 8, 1943, Melbourne, Florida, U.S.—died July 3, 1971, Paris, France), Ray Manzarek (born February 12, 1935, Chicago, Illinois), Robby Krieger (born January 8, 1946, Los Angeles, California), and John Densmore (born December 1, 1945, Los Angeles).

The Doors' instrumentalists— keyboardist Manzarek, guitarist Krieger, and drummer Densmore— combined backgrounds in classical music and blues with the improvisational daring of a jazz band. It was the dark-edged eroticism of Morrison's baritone and pseudo-poetic lyrics, however, that set the Los Angeles-based quartet apart from the prevailing hippie utopianism that pervaded West Coast rock in the late 1960s. Morrison's early death only enhanced his reputation as the quintessential rock showman and troubled artiste for subsequent generations.

Morrison's father was a naval officer (ultimately an admiral), and though the family moved frequently, it settled down in the Washington, D.C., suburb of Alexandria, Virginia, where Morrison attended high school and was a good but rebellious student. After beginning his college education at Florida State University, he transferred to the University of California, Los Angeles, to study film. There he met Ray Manzarek.

The two conceived the group after the singer recited one of his poems to the keyboardist on a southern California beach. Morrison took the band's name from Aldous Huxley's book on mescaline, *The Doors of Perception*, which in turn referred to a line in a poem by William Blake. The Doors acquired a reputation for pushing the boundaries of rock composition, both musically and lyrically, in performances on the Sunset

Strip in Los Angeles. Their breakthrough hit, "Light My Fire," was an anthem in 1967, but it was songs such as "The End"—an 11-minute Oedipal drama with sexually explicit lyrics and a swirling, ebb-and-flow arrangement—that established the Doors' reputation as one of rock's most potent, controversial, and theatrical acts. Indeed, the group was banned from the Whisky-A-Go-Go in Los Angeles after an early performance of the song.

Though the group's ambitious music encompassed everything from Chicago blues to German cabaret, their string of pop hits caused them to be dismissed by some critics as a teenybopper act; this deeply troubled Morrison, who craved acceptance as a serious artist. By the time of the release of the Doors' third album, *Waiting for the Sun* (1968), Morrison had created a shamanistic alter ego for himself, the Lizard King; the singer's poem "The Celebration of the Lizard King" was printed inside the record jacket. His concert performances were marked by increasingly outrageous stunts, and Morrison was arrested in 1969 for exposing himself onstage in Miami. The charges were eventually dropped, but the incident served notice of Morrison's physical decline, in part because of his addiction to alcohol.

The singer took increasing solace in his poetry, some of which was published, and the group's tours became less frequent. The Doors reestablished their artistic credibility with the blues-steeped *Morrison Hotel* (1970), but after the quartet's sixth studio release, *L.A. Woman* (1971), Morrison retreated to Paris, where he hoped to pursue a literary career. Instead, he died there of heart failure in 1971 at age 27. Without Morrison, the Doors produced two undistinguished albums before breaking up. They reunited briefly in 1978 to record *An American Prayer*, providing backing music for poetry Morrison recorded before his death. Manzarek also produced albums for the punk band X.

In death Morrison was lionized by generations of fans, both as a youth icon and as an influence on singers such as Iggy Pop, Echo and the Bunnymen's Ian McCulloch, and Pearl Jam's Eddie Vedder. The Doors' releases have continued to sell in the millions, and *The Doors*, a 1991 movie directed by Oliver Stone, was a critical and popular success. The Doors were inducted into the Rock and Roll Hall of Fame in 1993.

THE 13TH FLOOR ELEVATORS

The 13th Floor Elevators from Austin, Texas, epitomized the darker, more psychotic frenzy of acid rock. Featuring the wayward talent of Roky Erickson, a gifted musician and songwriter who was later hospitalized for mental illness, the band played visionary jug-blowing blues. The track "Slip Inside This House," for instance, on *Easter Everywhere* (1967), conveys a sense of mysticism and transcendence, enhanced by acid. Erickson's occult explorations took him so far that by the time the band split in 1969, he believed Satan was following him everywhere.

JIMI HENDRIX

Jimi Hendrix, along with the space-age funk of Parliament, was the key connection between psychedelia and black music. Guitarist, singer, and composer Hendrix (born November 27, 1942, Seattle, Washington, U.S.—died September 18, 1970, London, England) fused American traditions of blues, jazz, rock, and soul with techniques of British avant-garde rock to redefine the electric guitar in his own image.

Though his active career as a featured artist lasted a mere four years, Hendrix altered the course of popular music and became one of the most successful and influential musicians of his era. An instrumentalist who radically redefined the expressive potential and sonic palette of the electric guitar, he was the composer of a classic repertoire of songs ranging from ferocious rockers to delicate, complex ballads. He also was the most charismatic in-concert performer of his generation. Moreover, he was a visionary who collapsed the genre boundaries of rock, soul, blues, and jazz and an iconic figure whose appeal linked the concerns of white hippies and black revolutionaries by clothing black anger in the colourful costumes of London's Carnaby Street.

A former paratrooper whose honourable medical discharge exempted him from service in the Vietnam War, Hendrix spent the early 1960s working as a freelance accompanist for a variety of musicians, both famous and obscure. His unorthodox style and penchant for playing at high volume, however, limited him to subsistence-level work until he was discovered in a small New York City club and brought to England in August 1966. Performing alongside two British musicians, bassist Noel Redding and drummer Mitch Mitchell, he stunned London's clubland with his instrumental virtuosity and extroverted showmanship, numbering members of the Beatles, the Rolling Stones, and the Who among his admirers. It proved a lot easier for him to learn their tricks than it was for them to learn his.

Hendrix had an encyclopaedic knowledge of the musical roots on which the cutting-edge rock of his time was based, but, thanks to his years on the road with the likes of

Jimi Hendrix performing at the Monterey Pop Festival in 1967. Michael Ochs Archives/Getty Images

Little Richard and the Isley Brothers, he also had hands-on experience of the cultural and social worlds in which those roots had developed and a great admiration for the work of Bob Dylan, the Beatles, and the Yardbirds. Speedily adapting the current musical and sartorial fashions of late 1966 London to his own needs, he was soon able not only to match the likes of the Who at their own high-volume, guitar-smashing game but also to top them with what rapidly became the hottest-ticket show in town.

By November his band, the Jimi Hendrix Experience, had their first Top Ten single, "Hey Joe." Two more hits, "Purple Haze" and "The Wind Cries Mary," followed before their first album, *Are You Experienced?*, was released in the summer of 1967, when it was second in impact only to the Beatles' *Sgt. Pepper's Lonely Hearts Club Band*. Its immediate successor, *Axis: Bold as Love*, followed that December. On Paul McCartney's recommendation, Hendrix was flown to California for a scene-stealing appearance at the Monterey Pop Festival, which rendered him a sensation in his homeland less than a year after his departure.

Relocating back to the United States in 1968, he enjoyed further acclaim with the sprawling, panoramic double album *Electric Ladyland*, but the second half of his career proved frustrating. Legal complications from an old contract predating his British sojourn froze his recording royalties, necessitating constant touring to pay his bills; and his audiences were reluctant to allow him to progress beyond the musical blueprint of his earliest successes. He was on the verge of solving both these problems when he died of an overdose of barbiturates, leaving behind a massive stockpile of works-in-progress that were eventually edited and completed by others.

For Hendrix, the thunderous drama of his hard rock band was but a fraction of what he aspired to: he wanted to compose more complex music for larger ensembles, rather than simply to improvise endlessly in front of a rhythm section for audiences waiting for him to smash or burn his guitar. Nevertheless, in his all-too-brief career, he managed to combine and extend the soaring improvisational transcendence of John Coltrane, the rhythmic virtuosity of James Brown, the bluesy intimacy of John Lee Hooker, the lyrical aesthetic of Bob Dylan, the bare-knuckle onstage aggression of the Who, and the hallucinatory studio fantasias of the Beatles. Hendrix's work provides a continuing source of inspiration to successive generations of musicians to whom he remains a touchstone for emotional honesty, technological innovation, and an all-inclusive vision of cultural and social brotherhood.

LUCY IN THE SKY AND GOOD VIBRATIONS

Established rock bands began to introduce psychedelic elements into their music, notably the Beatles, with such records as *Revolver* (1966), featuring the pounding mantra of "Tomorrow Never Knows"; *Sgt. Pepper's Lonely Hearts Club Band* (1967), with the trippy lyrics of "Lucy in the Sky with Diamonds"; *Magical Mystery Tour* (1967), showcasing the swirling surrealism of songs like "Strawberry Fields Forever" and "I Am the Walrus"; and *The Beatles* (1968; the "White Album"), containing the standout track "Revolution 9," an experimental collage of found sounds.

The Beach Boys, too, branched out with the expansive, haunting *Pet Sounds* (1966), an album masterminded by an introspective Brian Wilson. The Yardbirds, with Jeff Beck on guitar, scored a hit with the echo-laden "Shapes of Things" (1966). Encouraged by Brian Jones, who was drawn to instruments like the sitar and ancient Eastern percussion, the Rolling Stones dipped their feet into the scene with songs like "Paint It Black" (1966) and the less-successful album *Their Satanic Majesties Request* (1967).

BRITISH PSYCHEDELIA

In Britain psychedelic pioneers created music that was steeped in whimsy and surrealism and was less aggressive and minimalist than their American counterparts. The scene revolved around venues such as London's UFO club (a predecessor to festivals like Glastonbury) and Middle Earth and such events as the 14-Hour Technicolor Dream, a happening in April 1967 in the Alexandra Palace that featured an enormous pile of bananas and bands like Pink Floyd, the Crazy World of Arthur Brown, and the Utterly Incredible Too Long Ago to Remember Sometimes Shouting at People. A benefit for the alternative newspaper *IT* (*International Times*), the event also drew counterculture celebrities such as John Lennon, Yoko Ono, and Andy Warhol.

PINK FLOYD

Pink Floyd was the leading light of the British underground scene, with vocalist-guitarist Syd Barrett the main writer behind such hits as "Arnold Layne" (a quirky, controversial song about a transvestite) and the spacey, driving instrumental "Interstellar Overdrive." He was a strong creative force until his worsening schizophrenia led to him being edged out of the band in 1968. In addition to Barrett (born Roger Keith Barrett, January 6, 1946, Cambridge, Cambridgeshire, England—died July 7, 2006, Cambridge), the principal members were bassist Roger Waters (born September 6, 1943, Great Bookham, Surrey), drummer Nick Mason (born January 27, 1945, Birmingham, West Midlands), keyboard player Rick Wright (born July 28, 1945, London—died September 15, 2008, London), and guitarist David Gilmour (born March 6, 1944, Cambridge).

Formed in 1965, the band went through several name changes before combining the first names of a pair of Carolina bluesmen, Pink Anderson and Floyd Council. Their initial direction came from vocalist-guitarist-songwriter Barrett, whose mixture of blues, music hall styles,

159

Lewis Carroll references, and dissonant psychedelia established the band as a cornerstone of the British underground scene. They signed with EMI and early in 1967 had their first British hit with the controversial "Arnold Layne." This was followed by their debut album, *The Piper at the Gates of Dawn*, a lush, experimental record that has since become a rock classic. Their sound was becoming increasingly adventurous, incorporating sound effects, spacy guitar and keyboards, and extended improvisation such as "Interstellar Overdrive."

By 1968 Barrett, who had overused LSD and was struggling with schizophrenia, was replaced by guitarist Gilmour. Without Barrett's striking lyrics, the band moved away from the singles market to concentrate on live work, continuing its innovations in sound and lighting but with varying degrees of success. After recording a series of motion-picture soundtrack albums, they entered the American charts with *Atom Heart Mother* (1970) and *Meddle* (1971). Making records that were song-based but thematic in approach and that included long instrumental passages, the band did much to popularize the concept album. They hit the commercial jackpot with *Dark Side of the Moon* (1973). A bleak treatise on death and emotional breakdown underlined by Waters's dark songwriting, it sent Pink Floyd soaring into the megastar bracket and remained in the American pop charts for more than a decade. The follow-up, *Wish You Were Here* (1975), included "Shine On You Crazy Diamond," a song for Barrett, and, though it went to number one in both the United States and Britain, it was considered anticlimactic and pompous by many critics.

By the release of *Animals* (1977), it was clear that Waters had become the band's dominant influence, and there was increasing internal conflict within Pink Floyd. Their sense of alienation (from both one another and contemporary society) was profoundly illustrated by the tour for 1979's best-selling album *The Wall*, for which a real brick wall was built between the group and the audience during performance. After the appropriately named *The Final Cut* (1983), Pink Floyd became inactive, and legal wrangles ensued over ownership of the band's name. Waters, who dismissed Wright after *The Wall* and took over most of the songwriting, was even more firmly in control. As a result the band split, but, much to Waters's chagrin, Gilmour, Mason, and Wright reunited, continuing as Pink Floyd. In the late 1980s Wright, Gilmour, and Mason released two albums, including the ponderous *A Momentary Lapse of Reason* (1987) and *The Division Bell* (1994), while Waters pursued a solo career. Waters reunited with his former bandmates for a single performance at the Live 8 benefit concert in 2005. Pink Floyd was inducted into the Rock and Roll Hall of Fame in 1996.

Other British acts included the anarchic Tomorrow, which specialized in droning raga feedback and wild drumming; the operatic, flamboyant Arthur Brown; the R&B-flavored Pretty Things; and the Canterbury band Soft Machine, which incorporated "harmolodic" jazz into their psychedelic rock.

IF YOU CAME TO SAN FRANCISCO

During the 1950s San Francisco supported several folk clubs including the hungry i, where the Kingston Trio recorded a best-selling live album in 1958. But the city was a backwater of the national music industry until 1966, when promoters such as Bill Graham began booking local bands at the Fillmore Auditorium and other large dance venues.

The Fillmore, along with the Avalon Ballroom, Fillmore West, and Winterland, ushered in the modern era of rock show presentation and grew out of the hippie counterculture of San Francisco's Haight-Ashbury district. The first multiband rock show was held at the Ark in Sausalito in 1965 and proved so successful that the presenters incorporated

their commune as the Family Dog shortly thereafter. Later that year Graham, the manager of the radical San Francisco Mime Troupe, organized a pair of rock concert benefit shows for the troupe. The first was held at the Calliope Ballroom on Howard Street and the second at the Fillmore Auditorium, a stylish ballroom at Geary and Fillmore streets on the outskirts of the city's black community. Inspired by the shows' success, Graham decided to go into the concert-promotion business, setting up operations at the Fillmore. At first Graham and the Family Dog shared the Fillmore, booking alternating weeks. Later Chet Helms, the Dog's booker, rented the Avalon Ballroom at 1268 Sutter, near the corner of Van Ness, and put it under the management of Bob Simmons, who had started the "underground rock" programming on KMPX-FM with Tom Donahue.

The formula for shows at these venues called for three bands per evening, originally playing two sets apiece. Graham often mixed genres in hopes of opening up his audiences' knowledge of music, whereas the Family Dog stuck mostly to its own favourite bands. In 1968 Graham also took over a larger and more central venue, the Carousel Ballroom, at the corner of Market and Van Ness. He renamed it the Fillmore West (so called because

TOM DONAHUE

As a Top 40 deejay in Philadelphia and San Francisco, "Big Daddy" Tom Donahue opened his show with a self-spoofing line: "I'm here to clean up your face and mess up your mind." But it was on the FM band in the late 1960s and '70s that Donahue changed the face—and sound—of radio. Along with a handful of others, Donahue invented free-form rock radio, in which hipster disc jockeys with a broad knowledge of music—usually extending beyond rock and into rhythm and blues, blues, jazz, folk, and country—played and said whatever they wanted.

Beginning at a lowly FM station, KMPX in San Francisco—where a deejay from Detroit, Larry Miller, was already playing an eclectic blend of music on the all-night shift—Donahue made free-form a commercial success. After a labour dispute, he and most of his staff moved to KSAN, a former classical station. One form of longhair music gave way to another, and KSAN became one of the most successful progressive rock stations in the country until the mid-1970s, when Donahue died (April 1975) and competing programmers came up with a mainstream version of free-form. This new format, album-oriented rock (AOR), meant the demise of free-form radio.

he had expanded his company, Bill Graham Presents, to New York City, where he operated the Fillmore East). When Graham closed the Fillmore West in 1971, he shifted operations to Winterland—a disused ice-skating rink at the corner of Steiner and Post streets—which he continued to use as his main small venue until urban renewal dictated its demolition in 1982. Winterland was the site of many significant rock events, not the least of which was the last live performance by the original members of the Band in 1976 (captured in the film *The Last Waltz*).

Graham, noted for his abrasive personality and hard-nosed business sense, proved to be far more successful than the Family Dog, which fell into disarray and moved its operations to Denver, Colorado. Indeed, Graham went on to become the most successful concert promoter in the United States, later moving into management (Santana, Journey, and other bands), merchandising (Winterland Productions was the first company to see the sales potential in official band-related T-shirts and other paraphernalia), and film production.

Graham had also been at the right place at the right time. The "local bands" that he began his concert promotion career booking just happened to include the Grateful Dead, the Jefferson Airplane, and Big Brother and the Holding Company, which was fronted by the premier white female blues vocalist of the 1960s, Janis Joplin.

JANIS JOPLIN

After an unhappy childhood in a middle-class family in southeastern Texas, Janis Joplin (born January 19, 1943 Port Arthur, Texas, U.S.—died October 4, 1970, Los Angeles, California) attended Lamar State College of Technology and the University of Texas at Austin before

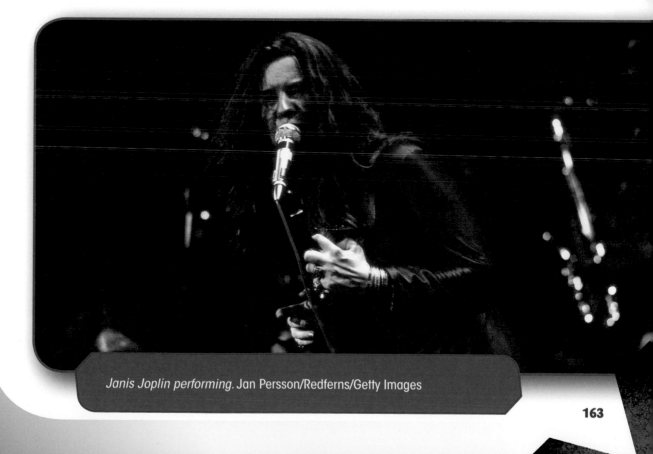

Janis Joplin performing. Jan Persson/Redferns/Getty Images

dropping out in 1963 to sing folk songs and especially the blues in Texas clubs. After a long sojourn in San Francisco (during which she abused alcohol and amphetamines), she went back to Texas, only to return to San Francisco in 1966 to become the vocalist for Big Brother and the Holding Company at the recommendation of Chet Helms. Buoyed by Joplin's raucous, bluesy vocals, the hard-rocking band released an album on independent Mainstream Records, then stunned audiences at the Monterey Pop Festival in 1967 with a legendary performance highlighted by Joplin's rendition of "Ball and Chain" (a rhythm-and-blues classic by Big Mama Thornton). Big Brother's first album for major label Columbia, *Cheap Thrills* (1968), went to number one (the single "Piece of My Heart" reached number 12), and onetime ugly duckling Joplin continued her transformation into a strong-willed, sexually aggressive rock icon.

Leaving Big Brother, she formed the Kozmic Blues Band, reaching number five in 1969 with *I Got Dem Ol' Kozmic Blues Again Mama!*. Joplin and the band performed at Woodstock but broke up shortly thereafter, and she became a regular heroin user. In 1970, engaged to be married, her life seemingly on track, Joplin was recording an album with her new group, the Full Tilt Boogie Band, when she died of an accidental overdose of heroin. Released posthumously, that album, *Pearl*, topped the chart in 1971, as did the single "Me and Bobby McGee." Joplin's importance in the history of rock is due not only to her strength as a singer but also to her intensity as a performer, which flew in the face of the conventions that dictated how a "girl singer" should act. Her raw blues-soaked voice—influenced by Thornton, Leadbelly, and Bessie Smith—was matched by her uninhibited physical movements. The two elements fused in a mesmerizing display of soulfulness few had thought a white singer could pull off. Joplin's story is presented in a thinly veiled biographical film, *The Rose* (1979). She was inducted into the Rock and Roll Hall of Fame in 1995.

CREEDENCE CLEARWATER REVIVAL

Most of the new local bands signed for huge advances with major out-of-town labels. The only local record label to survive was Fantasy Records, across the bay in Oakland, a predominantly jazz label that never tried to compete for the new drug-culture rock groups but outsold them all with the middle-American sound of Creedence Clearwater Revival. Derided by many rock critics at the time as merely a "singles" band, Creedence Clearwater

Revival proved to be masters at making thoughtful records that sold. The members were John Fogerty (born May 28, 1945, Berkeley, California, U.S.), Tom Fogerty (born November 9, 1941, Berkeley—died September 6, 1990, Scottsdale, Arizona), Stu Cook (born April 25, 1945, Oakland, California), and Doug Clifford (born April 24, 1945, Palo Alto, California).

John Fogerty and his brother Tom, both singer-guitarists, joined forces in 1959 with bassist Cook and drummer Clifford, their junior-high-school classmates in El Cerrito, California, a suburb in the San Francisco Bay area. After achieving marginal success under names such as the Blue Velvets and the Golliwogs, they emerged as Creedence Clearwater Revival in 1967, with John Fogerty as their lead singer, lead guitarist, and sole songwriter. Released on the Fantasy label, *Creedence Clearwater Revival* (1968) was marred by psychedelic clichés but nevertheless earned gold album status and yielded "Suzie Q (Parts 1 and 2)," which was a cover of the Dale Hawkins rock standard and reached number 11 on the American charts. This modest debut scarcely hinted at the power of their follow-up album, *Bayou Country* (1969), on which John Fogerty—singing with raw, grainy fervour and drawing inspiration from the wellspring of Southern rock and roll and blues—demonstrated his mastery of the three-minute rock song. "Proud Mary," a mythic journey down the Mississippi River of Fogerty's imagination, was an instant international hit.

Constant touring established Creedence as one of the era's most exciting live acts as Fogerty penned a remarkable string of hit singles. Along with creating driving dance tunes, he had an uncanny gift for catching the temper of the times that few of his peers could match. The hits "Bad Moon Rising" (1969) and "Who'll Stop the Rain" (1970) evoked the Vietnam War and civil discord without explicitly referring to those events; "Fortunate Son" (1969) was a furious blast at wealth and status. From the beginning of 1969 until the end of 1970, Creedence ruled the American pop charts. Their other albums from this period—*Green River* (1969), *Willy and the Poorboys* (1969), and *Cosmo's Factory* (1970)—collected hits such as "Green River," "Down on the Corner," "Up Around the Bend," and "Travelin' Band" (1970) and offered many other songs equal to them in craftsmanship.

Tom Fogerty left the band in 1971 as "Have You Ever Seen the Rain?" scaled the charts. Cook and Clifford demanded greater prominence, resulting in *Mardi Gras* (1972), which was dominated by their songs. Its critical and commercial failure led to the band's demise later that year. Unlike many 1960s acts, Creedence never staged a reunion. Tom Fogerty pursued a solo career until his death. Cook and Clifford worked as a rhythm section behind various artists before forming a touring version of Creedence with other musicians in 1995. John Fogerty's solo career was marred by legal battles over royalties (only later in his tenure as a solo artist would he consent to perform Creedence material) and by long intervals between albums; however, he topped the Billboard Top 200 albums chart in 1984 with *Centerfield*, won a Grammy Award in 1997 for *Blue Moon Swamp*, and delved into political songwriting again on *Deja Vu All Over Again* (2004) and *Revival* (2007). Creedence Clearwater Revival was inducted into the Rock and Roll Hall of Fame in 1993.

SANTANA

Another Bay Area band that did not fit comfortably under the psychedelic rock umbrella was Santana, whose use of salsa and mambo-style percussion exposed a wide rock audience to traditional Latin American music. The original members were Carlos Santana (born July 20, 1947, Autlán de Navarro, Mexico), Gregg Rolie (born June 17, 1947, Seattle, Washington, U.S.), David Brown (born February 15, 1947, New York), Mike Carabello (born November 18, 1947, San Francisco), José ("Chepito") Areas (born July 25, 1946, León, Nicaragua), and Mike Shrieve (born July 6, 1949, San Francisco).

Formed in 1966 in San Francisco, Santana leaped to prominence after its appearance at Woodstock in 1969. The same year, the group's debut album reached the Top Ten, and leader Carlos Santana joined the top echelon of rock guitarists. Santana's second album, *Abraxas* (1970), went to number one while spawning the hit singles "Black Magic Woman" and "Oye Como Va," and *Santana III* (1971), featuring new guitarist Neal Schon (born February 27, 1954, San Mateo, California). With *Caravanserai* (1972) the group shifted toward jazz. Musicians began leaving the band (which was inducted into the Rock and Roll Hall of Fame in 1998), most notably Rolie and Schon, who formed Journey. Influenced in part by the philosophy of Sri Chimnoy, Carlos Santana continued excursions into jazz-rock with various musicians for several years before returning, on *Amigos* (1976), to the formula that brought his initial success. *Moonflower*, a best-selling double album that included a hit remake of the Zombies' "She's Not There," followed in 1977.

Santana continued the pattern of alternating rock radio-friendly releases with jazz projects through the 1990s. In 1998 the group was inducted into the Rock and Roll Hall of Fame, and the following year Carlos Santana achieved the greatest commercial and critical success of his career with *Supernatural*, which included collaborations with such performers as Eric Clapton, Lauryn Hill, Dave Matthews, and Rob Thomas of Matchbox 20. The album topped the charts, selling more than 20 million copies, and received a record-tying eight Grammy Awards.

ROLLING STONE

Another essential element of the San Francisco scene was *Rolling Stone* magazine, founded in the city in 1967 by Jann Wenner, a former student at the University of California, Berkeley, and Ralph Gleason, a jazz critic for the *San Francisco Chronicle* newspaper. The first issue appeared on November 9, 1967, with John Lennon on the cover. The magazine's creators intended *Rolling Stone* to be a barometer of the artistic tastes and political sensibilities of the student generation. The magazine effectively combined passion and professionalism, using both proper English and "street language." Many well-known writers and journalists, including Hunter S. Thompson, Cameron Crowe, Lester Bangs, and Greil Marcus, started their careers with *Rolling Stone*. As the magazine increasingly came to define significant trends and discerning taste in rock and pop music, appearances on its cover were coveted by established as well as up-and-coming musicians as emblems of critical success. Along with the Beatles, Bob Dylan, Madonna, and many other musicians, *Rolling Stone*'s cover featured significant actors, writers, and politicians, such as Jack Nicholson, Susan Sontag, and Bill Clinton. In an effort to enhance its image, the magazine moved its offices to New York City in 1977.

In May 2006 *Rolling Stone* printed its 1,000th issue. Its success through the decades was due to its ability to adapt to constantly changing musical, political, and cultural climates. Issues of *Rolling Stone* typically include music and movie reviews, celebrity stories and photographs, information on new artists, fashion advice, and articles on politics. *Rolling Stone* has influenced pop culture through its "all-time greatest" lists, such as the "500 Greatest Albums of All Time" (issued in November 2003) and the "100 Greatest Singers of All Time" (issued in November 2008).

CHAPTER 12

Art Rockers

By the end of the 1960s the notion that rock and roll and art were compatible was gaining wider acceptance. Though other arguably thematically unified albums had preceded it, the Beatles' *Sgt. Pepper's Lonely Hearts Club Band* (1967) unquestionably brought the idea of the concept album to center stage in the pop music world. Among the other rockers who were the first to craft concept albums were the Who, most famously with the "rock operas" *Tommy* (1969) and *Quadrophenia* (1973), but even earlier with *The Who Sell Out* (1967), a faux pirate radio broadcast complete with fictitious commercials. The experimentalism of Pete Towshend, the driving force behind the Who, no doubt had much to do with his experience as an art student. Indeed, a number of Townshend's contemporaries, notably John Lennon, Keith Richard, and Eric Clapton, attended art schools, which continued to exert an important influence on the creation of rock music, especially in Britain (notably on the punk movement) but also in the United States.

In the 1970s the term *art rock* for many became synonymous with progressive rock, the classically influenced, "intellectual" rock made by groups such as Yes, Genesis, and King Crimson, but it also remained associated with the experimental work created by decidedly unconventional performers such as the Velvet Underground, Frank Zappa, and Captain Beefheart and his Magic Band. Initially the Velvet

Underground was guided by pop artist Andy Warhol, and the group developed in the hothouse creative environment of Warhol's Factory in New York City. Album art (the images on record sleeves) also became an increasingly important element of the rock music package, and Warhol contributed the now-familiar banana cover for the band's debt album, *The Velvet Underground and Nico* (1966). (He also created the album cover for the Rolling Stones' *Sticky Fingers*, while British pop artist Peter Blake had been responsible for the Beatles inventive *Sgt. Pepper*'s cover.)

THE VELVET UNDERGROUND

The Velvet Underground's primal guitar sound and urban-noir lyrics, influenced by avant-garde art and modern literature, inspired the punk and alternative rock movements of the 1970s and '80s. The principal members were Lou Reed (born Lewis Alan Reed, March 2, 1942, New York, New York, U.S.), John Cale (born March 9, 1942, Garnant, Wales), Sterling Morrison (born Holmes Sterling Morrison, August 29, 1942, Westbury, New York—died August 30, 1995, Poughkeepsie, New York), Maureen ("Moe") Tucker (born August 26, 1944, Levittown, Long Island, New York), Nico (born Christa Päffgen, October 16, 1938, Cologne, Germany—died 18, 1988, Ibiza, Spain), Angus MacLise, and Doug Yule.

The son of an accountant, Reed grew up on Long Island, New York, made his first record at age 14 (as a member of the Shades), and studied literature and drama at Syracuse (New York) University, where he came under the influence of poet Delmore Schwartz.

Trained as a classical musician in London, Welshman Cale came to the United States in 1963 on a Leonard Bernstein scholarship to study composition but soon joined the Dream Syndicate, a pioneering minimalist ensemble founded in New York City by La Monte Young. In 1965, while working as a Brill Building-style staff songwriter for Pickwick Music, Reed formed a group, the Primitives (including Cale), for live performances of a single he had recorded called "The Ostrich." He also had written songs, such as "Heroin" and "Venus in Furs," that reflected his interest in the graphic, narrative realism of novelists Raymond Chandler and Hubert Selby, Jr. With guitarist Morrison (a Syracuse classmate of Reed's) and percussionist MacLise, Reed on guitar and vocals and Cale on piano, viola, and bass formed a more permanent band to play these songs, ultimately settling on the name the

The Velvet Underground. GAB Archive/Redferns/Getty Images

Velvet Underground, taken from the title of a paperback book about deviant sex.

The band performed live sound tracks for experimental films before making their formal debut, with new drummer Tucker, at a high school dance in December 1965. After seeing the group play in a Greenwich Village club, pop artist Andy Warhol became the Velvet Underground's manager and patron—introducing them to the exotic German actress, model, and chanteuse Nico; putting the group on tour with his performance art discotheque, the Exploding Plastic Inevitable; and financing and producing the Velvets' first album.

Recorded in 1966 but not released until the following year, *The Velvet Underground and Nico* was one of rock's most important debuts, a pioneering work that applied the disruptive aesthetics of avant-garde music and free jazz (drones, distortion, atonal feedback) to rock guitar. It also presented frank examinations of drug use, sadomasochism, and

DELMORE SCHWARTZ

American poet, short-story writer, and literary critic Delmore Schwartz (born December 8, 1913, Brooklyn, New York, U.S.— died July 11, 1966, New York, New York) was noted for his lyrical descriptions of cultural alienation and the search for identity. His first book, *In Dreams Begin Responsibilities* (1939), which brought him immediate fame, included the short story of the title and a group of poems remarkable for their lyric beauty and imaginative power. His subsequent publications included *Shenandoah* (1941), a verse play; *Genesis, Book I* (1943), a long introspective poem; *The World Is a Wedding* (1948) and *Successful Love, and Other Stories* (1961), short stories dealing primarily with middle-class Jewish family life. His lucid and sensitive literary criticism was published in various periodicals. His *New and Selected Poems, 1938–1958* appeared in 1959. Schwartz served as an editor for *Partisan Review* (1943–55) and *The New Republic* (1955–57). The brilliant but mentally unstable Schwartz was the model for the title character in Saul Bellow's novel *Humboldt's Gift* (1975).

numbing despair. At a time when the San Francisco scene represented the euphoric apex of 1960s counterculture, the Velvets' harsh dose of New York City-framed reality was scorned by the music industry and ignored by mainstream audiences.

The Velvet Underground's career was plagued by personal upheaval and financial struggle. Nico embarked on a solo career in 1967. Her unique style of ravishing melancholy was best captured on *Chelsea Girls* (1968), featuring contributions by Reed, Cale, and Morrison, and *The Marble Index* (1969), produced by Cale. Also in 1967, Reed dismissed Warhol as the group's manager. Cale was replaced by Doug Yule in 1968, after the release of *White Light/White Heat*, an album of extraordinary proto-punk ferocity. The 1950s rhythm-and-blues balladry

POP ART

The Pop art movement was largely a British and American cultural phenomenon of the late 1950s and '60s and was named by the art critic Lawrence Alloway in reference to the prosaic iconography of its painting and sculpture. Works by such Pop artists as the Americans Roy Lichtenstein, Andy Warhol, Claes Oldenburg, Tom Wesselman, James Rosenquist, and Robert Indiana and the Britons David Hockney and Peter Blake, among others, were characterized by their portrayal of any and all aspects of popular culture that had a powerful impact on contemporary life; their iconography—taken from television, comic books, movie magazines, and all forms of advertising—was presented emphatically and objectively, without praise or condemnation but with overwhelming immediacy, and by means of the precise commercial techniques used by the media from which the iconography itself was borrowed. Pop art represented an

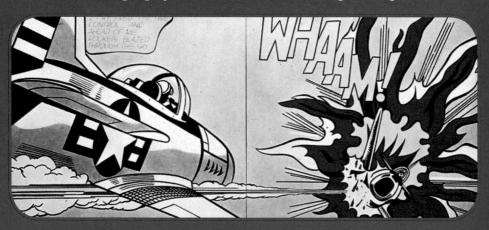

Whaam!, *acrylic and oil on two canvas panels by Roy Lichtenstein, 1963; in the Tate Modern, London. 174 × 408 cm.* Courtesy of the trustees of the Tate Gallery, London

George Segal, with one of his works, photograph by Arnold Newman, 1964. © Arnold Newman

attempt to return to a more objective, universally acceptable form of art after the dominance in both the United States and Europe of the highly personal Abstract Expressionism. It was also iconoclastic, rejecting both the supremacy of the "high art" of the past and the pretensions of other contemporary avant-garde art. Pop art became a cultural event because of its close reflection of a particular social situation and because its easily comprehensible images were immediately exploited by the mass media. Although the critics of Pop art described it as vulgar, sensational, nonaesthetic, and a joke, its proponents (a minority in the art world) saw it as an art that was democratic and nondiscriminatory, bringing together both connoisseurs and untrained viewers.

Pop art was a descendant of Dada, a nihilistic movement current in the 1920s that ridiculed the seriousness of contemporary Parisian art and, more broadly, the political and cultural situation that had brought war to Europe. Marcel Duchamp, the champion of Dada in the United States, who tried to narrow the distance between art and life by celebrating the mass-produced objects of his time, was the most influential figure in the evolution of Pop art. The immediate predecessors of the Pop artists were Jasper Johns, Larry Rivers, and Robert Rauschenberg, American artists who in the 1950s painted flags, beer cans, and other similar objects, though with a painterly, expressive technique.

Some of the more striking forms that Pop art took were Roy Lichtenstein's stylized reproductions of comic strips using the colour dots and flat tones of commercial printing; Andy Warhol's meticulously literal paintings and silk-screen prints of soup-can labels, soap cartons, and rows of soft-drink bottles; Claes Oldenburg's soft plastic sculptures of objects such as bathroom fixtures, typewriters, and gigantic hamburgers.

Most Pop artists aspired to an impersonal, urbane attitude in their works. Some examples of Pop art, however, were subtly expressive of social criticism—for example, Oldenburg's drooping objects and Warhol's monotonous repetitions of the same banal image have an undeniably disturbing effect—and some, such as sculptor George Segal's mysterious, lonely tableaux, are overtly expressionistic.

American Pop art tended to be emblematic, anonymous, and aggressive; English Pop, more subjective and referential, expressed a somewhat romantic view of Pop culture fostered perhaps by England's relative distance from it. English Pop artists tended to deal with technology and popular culture primarily as themes, even metaphors; some American Pop artists actually seemed to live these ideas. Warhol's motto, for example, was, "I think everybody should be a machine," and he tried in his art to produce works that a machine would have made.

and pop classicism that subtly flavoured Reed's songwriting blossomed on *The Velvet Underground* (1969) and *Loaded* (1970). But the strain of commercial failure led Reed to quit in August 1970. A version of the band led by Yule limped into the early 1970s.

As solo artists, Reed and Cale introduced the Velvet Underground's vision and legacy to a wider audience. Reed had an overdue hit in 1972 with the album *Transformer*; coproduced by Velvets admirer David Bowie, it featured "Walk on the Wild Side," which reached number 16 on the American pop chart. He then established himself as a punk-godfather figure with releases such as the lavish song suite *Berlin* (1973), the feedback oratorio *Metal Machine Music* (1975), and the concept album *New York* (1989). In addition to his own pop and rock solo recordings, Cale produced and collaborated with Velvet Underground-influenced artists such as Iggy and the Stooges, Jonathan Richman, Brian Eno, and Patti Smith; Cale also composed and released numerous orchestral works and movie scores. In 1989 Reed and Cale reunited to write and record *Songs for Drella*, an eloquent requiem for their mentor Warhol.

Morrison and Tucker left the Reed-less Velvet Underground in 1971. Morrison studied medieval literature, then worked as a tugboat captain. Tucker, whose African-heartbeat style of drumming made her an underground-rock icon, raised a family and made occasional solo records. On June 15, 1990, at a celebration of Warhol's art and life in France, Reed, Cale, Morrison, and Tucker performed together for the first time since 1968; they toured Europe in 1993 and recorded a concert album before breaking up again. In 1996 the Velvet Underground were inducted into the Rock and Roll Hall of Fame.

CAPTAIN BEEFHEART

Performing with the shifting lineup of musicians known as His Magic Band, avant-garde rock and blues singer, songwriter, and instrumentalist Captain Beefheart (born Don Van Vliet, January 15, 1941, Glendale, California, U.S.—died December 17, 2010, Arcata, California) produced a series of albums from the 1960s to the '80s that had limited commercial appeal but were a major influence on punk and experimental rock.

A child prodigy as a sculptor, Beefheart grew up in the Mojave Desert region of California, where he and Frank Zappa met as teenagers. Having learned to play the harmonica and saxophone, Beefheart formed the first Magic Band in 1964, and the group (which briefly included Ry Cooder) had moderate success with the albums *Safe as Milk* (1967) and *Strictly Personal* (1968). Beefheart's most famous recording, *Trout Mask Replica* (1969), produced by Zappa, proved an astonishing departure from previous rock conventions, combining eerie slide guitars, unpredictable rhythms, and surrealistic lyrics that Beefheart (who possessed a five-octave range) wailed with fierce intensity. His songs conveyed a deep distrust of modern civilization, a yearning for ecological balance, and the belief that animals in the wild are far superior to human beings. Although he won critical acclaim with *Clear Spot* (1972), *Shiny Beast (Bat Chain Puller)* (1978), *Ice Cream for Crow* (1982), and other albums, Beefheart never won a wide popular following; however, his music greatly influenced such groups as the Clash and Devo. In the early 1980s Beefheart, again using the name Don Van Vliet, left the music business altogether and devoted himself to painting. He died in December 2010 of complications from multiple sclerosis.

FRANK ZAPPA

Frank Zappa (born December 21, 1940, Baltimore, Maryland, U.S.—died December 4, 1993, Los Angeles, California) was, in no apparent order, a first-rate cultural gadfly dedicated to upsetting American suburban complacency and puncturing the hypocrisy and pretensions of both the U.S. political establishment and the counterculture that opposed it; a contemporary orchestral composer uncompromisingly rooted in 20th-century avant-garde tradition; a rock bandleader who put together a series of stellar ensembles both under the rubric of the Mothers of Invention and under his own name; an erudite lover of the most esoteric traditions of rock and roll and of rhythm and blues; an innovative record producer whose use of high-speed editing techniques predated the later innovations of hip-hop; and one of the premier electric guitar improvisers of a generation that included Jimi Hendrix, Eric Clapton, and Jeff Beck. One of the great polymaths of the rock era who, arguably, possessed a broader range of skills and interests than any of his peers, he was an instinctive postmodernist who demolished the barriers and hierarchies separating "high" and "low" culture.

Zappa was a prolific workaholic who released more than 60 albums in his 30-year career. His first release with the original Mothers of Invention, the conceptual double album *Freak Out!* (1966), was a key influence on the Beatles' *Sgt. Pepper's Lonely Hearts Club Band*, released the following year. By way of wry acknowledgment, the cover of the Mothers' third album, *We're Only in It for the Money* (1967), parodied that of *Sgt. Pepper's*, just as the music challenged the Beatles' visions of love and beauty with the deliberate "ugliness" with which Zappa assailed what he saw as the totalitarian philistinism of the establishment and the vacuous fatuity of many aspects of hippie subculture. Zappa was not a hippie, he claimed. He was a "freak."

After retiring the name the Mothers of Invention in the late 1970s, Zappa withdrew from explicit political commentary and released, under his own name, the enormously influential jazz-rock fusion album *Hot Rats* (1969), which featured a memorable vocal from his old friend Don Van Vliet, better known as Captain Beefheart. Throughout the 1970s Zappa released instrumental albums that featured orchestral music, jazz, his own guitar improvisations, and, later, synthesizers and sequencers. He also released rock-oriented vocal albums that, like most of his live concerts, specialized in jaw-dropping displays of technical virtuosity and crowd-pleasing exercises in misogynistic grossness such as "Titties & Beer" (1978) and "Jewish Princess" (1979)

In the 1980s, by contrast, Zappa was sufficiently angered by the policies of U.S. President Ronald Reagan's administration to rediscover politics. He set up voter-registration booths in the lobbies of his concerts and memorably testified against censorship at the Parents' Music Resource Center hearings in 1985 in Washington, D.C. In 1982 he had an unlikely hit single with "Valley Girl," which featured a rap by his daughter Moon Unit; and, shortly before his death from prostate cancer in 1993, he was finally recognized as a composer of "serious" music when his Yellow Shark suite was performed and recorded by Berlin's Ensemble Modern. Zappa was posthumously honoured when a set of his pieces was performed during the Proms festival at London's Royal Albert Hall. Considering that he had been banned from the Albert Hall in 1970 when the theatre manager objected to some of the saltier lyrics from Zappa's motion picture *200 Motels* (1971), this was no mean achievement. Zappa was inducted into the Rock and Roll Hall of Fame in 1995.

Conclusion

Like politics, American popular music is an ongoing conversation between the present and the past. This was perhaps never more evident than in the 1960s. The musicians of the folk revival, both in the United States and Britain, mined the treasure trove of their national folk and popular musics, some of the most imaginative of which might too easily have been forgotten had it not been collected and stored in the warehouse of Harry Smith's *Anthology of American Folk Music* or the Lomaxes' Library of Congress recordings. But even as they were excavating the past, these musicians were reinventing it, embracing traditional forms but reshaping them to meet the needs, politics, aesthetics, technology, and marketing model of the moment. In the process, they created their own golden era.

It may be the most interesting twist (and shout) of the period that it took an invasion of British musicians to remind Americans of the tremendous vitality and potential of their indigenous rock and roll and rhythm and blues. In less than a decade, many, if not most, young Americans had lost sight of the sensual, romantic, and rebellious power of early rockers such as Elvis Presley, Chuck Berry, Little Richard, and Buddy Holly. The Beatles and Rolling Stones, among others, reminded them, moving importantly beyond homage to create their own form of rock and roll, rooted in their songwriting and style (both musically and in the way they moved through the world). Bob Dylan showed the Beatles and everyone else that sophisticated poetry and pop music could form a potent partnership. The Beatles showed the Byrds—as well as other early folk rockers—and reminded Dylan (who had rocked as a teenager) that electrification plus eloquence equaled excitement. The Rolling Stones reinvested the blues in rock. Rhythm and blues recast itself profoundly as soul, borrowing from gospel to marry the sacred and the profane in one of the most expressive and emotional forms of popular music ever.

At a time of war and social upheaval, the politics of civil rights, freedom, and peace came along for the ride and for more than a while drove the bus. Social change, rock, and soul were all part of the same stew. Lifestyle, fashion, and listening choices were political statements. Youth became a social class. The pursuit of enlightenment and thrills through the use of hallucinogenic drugs was widespread and came with its own psychedelic wardrobe, vocabulary, and soundtrack. Sexual liberation was everywhere. All that was needed was love, or so sang the Beatles.

A change had most definitely come; however, as the decade closed with the politics of reaction pushing back hard and capitalism co-opting much of the counterculture, rebellion became increasingly less a component of the sex, drugs, and rock-and-roll lifestyle and philosophy. Self-discovery and self-involvement became the cornerstones for many in the 1970s, which Tom Wolfe, who had been there for the Acid Tests, famously characterized as the "Me Decade." Popular music's most telling analog would be the ascendancy of the confessional poetics of the singer-songwriters. Moreover, the music industry, already a very big business by the end of the 1960s, would become exponentially bigger and, in the eyes of many, less vital. Yet the seeds for later rebellion had been sown, not least by the arty iconoclasm of the Velvet Underground. It is one of rock history's most revisited conceits that while the Velvets did not sell many records in their heyday, everyone who saw them play formed a band. Some of those bands would go on to change the landscape of rock music yet again in the 1970s.

Glossary

agitprop Political propaganda promulgated chiefly in literature, drama, music, or art.

archetype The original pattern or model of which all things of the same type are representations or copies.

arpeggio Production of the tones of a chord in succession and not simultaneously.

avatar An embodiment (as of a concept or philosophy) often in a person.

beatnik Mainstream term for a person who participated in a social movement of the 1950s and early 1960s which stressed artistic self-expression and the rejection of the mores of conventional society.

bohemian A person (as a writer or an artist) living an unconventional life often in a colony with others.

broadside ballad A descriptive or narrative verse or song, commonly in a simple ballad form, on a popular theme, and sung or recited in public places or printed on sheets called broadsides for sale in the streets.

chitlin circuit A group of segregation-era theatres and nightclubs that catered to African American audiences and featured black entertainers. Also used to refer to contemporary clubs with a similar focus.

counterculture In the late 1960s, a culture that emerged reflecting the rebellious attitudes of a young, college-educated population who exchanged their parents' traditions for an eclectic set of values woven from four distinct sources: politics, sex, drugs, and music.

demotic Popular; common.

dirge A slow, solemn, and mournful piece of music.

distortion Falsified reproduction of an audio or video signal caused by change in the wave form of the original signal.

dithyrambic Of or relating to a usually short poem in an inspired wild irregular strain.

donnybrook A usually public quarrel or dispute; free-for-all.

Dust Bowl A section of the Great Plains of the United States—extending over southeastern Colorado, southwestern Kansas, the panhandles of Texas and Oklahoma, and northeastern New Mexico—that faced overcultivation, drought, and dust storms in the 1930s.

franchise The right to vote.

free-form radio Radio format in which disc jockeys were allowed to choose their own records, usually rooted in rock but ranging from jazz and blues to country and folk music as well. They had similar latitude with nonmusical elements, including interviews, newscasts, and impromptu live performances.

hootenanny A gathering at which folksingers entertain often with the audience joining in.

iconoclasm The doctrine, practice, or attitude of someone who attacks settled beliefs or institutions.

McCarthyism A mid-20th century political attitude characterized chiefly by opposition to elements held to be subversive and by the use of tactics involving personal attacks on individuals by means of widely publicized indiscriminate allegations especially on the basis of unsubstantiated charges.

melisma A group of notes or tones sung on one syllable in plainsong.

mod Of, relating to, or being the characteristic style of 1960s British youth culture.

modal Of or relating to any of several ways of ordering the notes of a scale according to the intervals they form with the tonic, thus providing a theoretical framework for the melody.

New Left A political movement originating especially among students in the 1960s, favoring confrontational tactics, often breaking with older leftist ideologies, and concerned especially with antiwar, antinuclear, feminist, and ecological issues.

nihilism A viewpoint that traditional values and beliefs are unfounded and that existence is senseless and useless.

patois A dialect other than the standard or literary dialect.

raga In the classical music of India, Bangladesh, and Pakistan, a melodic framework for improvisation and composition that is based on a scale with a given set of notes, a typical order in which they appear in melodies, and characteristic musical motifs.

reverb An electronically produced echo effect in recorded music.

skiffle Style of music played on rudimentary instruments, first popularized in the United States in the 1920s but revived by British musicians in the mid-1950s.

tatterdemalion Ragged or disreputable in appearance.

Bibliography

THE BEATLES

The Beatles Anthology (2000) is the band's official autobiography and contains numerous anecdotes and quotes as well as previously unpublished photographs. The definitive summary of the basic facts is presented in Mark Lewisohn, *The Complete Beatles Chronicles* (1992). Bob Spitz, *The Beatles: The Biography* (2005), is readable and comprehensive. The best account of Beatlemania, written while it was happening, is Michael Braun, *Love Me Do: The Beatles' Progress* (1964, reissued 1995). Hunter Davies, The Beatles, 2nd rev. ed. (1996, reissued 2010), is a longtime authorized account. Two useful biographies are by longtime London music writers: Ray Coleman, *John Winston Lennon* (1984), and *John Ono Lennon* (1984), published together as *Lennon* (1984); and Barry Miles, *Paul McCartney: Many Years from Now* (1997). The best musical analysis is Ian MacDonald, *Revolution in the Head: The Beatles' Records and the Sixties*, 2nd rev. ed. (2005).

THE ROLLING STONES

The story of the Rolling Stones is told most effectively in Stanley Booth, *The True Adventures of the Rolling Stones* (1985, reissued 2000, originally published as *Dance with the Devil: The Rolling Stones and Their Times*); though Victor Bockris, *Keith Richards: The Biography* (1998), has much to recommend it; and Philip Norman, *The Life and Good Times of the Rolling Stones* (1989), is undeniably solid and workmanlike. Keith Richards, *Life* (2010), presents the author's side of life inside the Rolling Stones circus.

THE KINKS

Jon Savage, *The Kinks: The Official Biography* (1984), is a well-illustrated work. Ray Davies, *X-Ray* (1994, reissued in 2007 with a new introduction), presents the author's satiric look at his career.

THE WHO

Gary Herman, *The Who* (1972), an early biography, offers useful cultural background and insights. Dave Marsh, *Before I Get Old: The Story of the Who* (1983), is much more detailed but loses interest in the group after Keith Moon's death. Billed as a visual history, Richard Barnes, *The Who: Maximum R&B*, rev. ed (1996), offers an insider's perspective as well as extraordinary images. Keith Moon has been the subject of several books, including Dougal Butler, *Full Moon* (also published as *Moon the Loon*, 1981), a vivid ramble of recollections by his personal assistant. Tony Fletcher, *Moon: The Life and Death of a Rock Legend* (1998), is far more ambitious and credible.

BOB DYLAN

Daniel Kramer, *Bob Dylan* (1967), is primarily a book of photos by the photographer who had the least-restricted access to Dylan at crucial moments. Anthony Scaduto, *Bob Dylan* (1971, reissued 2001), is the earliest biography, though not the best. Robert Alexander and Michael Gross, *Bob Dylan: An Illustrated History* (1978), another comparatively early biography, is opinionated but sprinkled with interesting photos and fairly accurate. Jonathan Cott, *Dylan* (1984), is a masterful collection of photos and a smattering of high-concept text in an oversize coffee-table book from the publishers of *Rolling Stone*. Years in the making, Robert Shelton, *No Direction Home: The Life and Music of Bob Dylan* (1986, reprinted 1997), is the most ambitious of the biographies but ultimately lacks focus. (A revised and updated edition was released in 2011.)

Bob Spitz, *Dylan: A Biography* (1989, reprinted 1991), is the most accurate and readable. Unlike the gossipy accounts of other writers who have obsessed about Dylan, Paul Williams, *Performing Artist: The Music of Bob Dylan, The Early Years, 1960–1973* (1990), *Bob Dylan: Performing Artist: The Middle Years, 1974–1986* (1992), and *Bob Dylan: Performing Artist: 1986–1990 & Beyond: Mind Out of Time* (2004), present serious studies of Dylan's life and work. Richard Williams, *Dylan: A Man Called Alias* (1992), another oversize compendium, presents a less-arresting collection of photos than Cott's *Dylan* but offers an Englishman's perspective that is academic and sobering. Al Kooper, *Backstage Passes & Backstabbing Bastards: Memoirs of a Rock 'n' Roll Survivor* (1998), presents a firsthand account of many of the most pivotal moments in Dylan's career.

Perhaps the most informative of more recent biographies of Dylan is Howard Sounes, *Down the Highway: The Life of Bob Dylan* (2001). David Hajdu, *Positively 4th Street: The Lives and Times of Joan Baez, Bob Dylan,*

Mimi Baez Farina and Richard Farina (2001), examines the intersection of Dylan's life with those of three early intimates. Mike Marqusee, *Chimes of Freedom: The Politics of Bob Dylan's Art* (2003), focuses Dylan's work in a political context. Christopher Ricks, *Dylan's Visions of Sin* (2003), is a consideration of Dylan's oeuvre from a literary perspective by a scholar known best for his examination of English poetry and English poets. Clinton Heylin, *Revolution in the Air: The Songs of Bob Dylan, 1957–1973* (2009), is a comprehensive chronological account of Dylan's song output over a 17-year period. Much more specific in its focus is Greil Marcus, *Like a Rolling Stone: Bob Dylan at the Crossroads*, which pinpoints Dylan at arguably the apex of his creative genius. Greil Marcus, *Bob Dylan by Greil Marcus: Writings 1968–2010* (2010), collects the author's extensive writings on Dylan.

FOLK AND FOLK ROCK

The development of the folk rock revival is the subject of Ronald D. Cohen, *Rainbow Quest: The Folk Music Revival and American Society, 1940–1970* (2002); and Robert Cantwell, *When We Were Good: The Folk Revival* (1996). An audacious meditation on a classic album, Greil Marcus, *The Old, Weird America: The World of Bob Dylan's Basement Tapes* (2001, previously published as *Invisible Republic: Bob Dylan's Basement Tapes*), tries to capture an elusive essence of American roots music.

THE BAND

Levon Helm and Stephen Davis, *This Wheel's on Fire: Levon Helm and the Story of the Band* (1993), is a racy, from-the-horse's-mouth account of the group's rise and flameout; however, it is marred by its considerable enmity toward Robbie Robertson. Barney Hoskyns, *Across the Great Divide: The Band and America* (1993), is, at the very least, a more detached view of the group's dynamic and perhaps a more focused celebration of its musical achievement.

SOUL MUSIC

Peter Guralnick, *Sweet Soul Music: Rhythm and Blues and the Southern Dream of Freedom* (1986, reprinted 2002), gives a comprehensive overview of the movement. Jerry Wexler and David Ritz, *Rhythm and the Blues: A Life in American Music* (1993), is written from producer Wexler's point of view.

JAMES BROWN

James Brown and Bruce Tucker, *James Brown: The Godfather of Soul* (1986, reissued 2002), is his autobiography. Gerri Hirshey, *Nowhere to Run: The Story of Soul Music* (1984, reissued 1994), pp. 54–63, contains information based on interviews with Brown.

ARETHA FRANKLIN

Franklin's career is discussed in Peter Guralnick, *Sweet Soul Music: Rhythm and Blues and the Southern Dream of Freedom* (1986, reprinted 2002), pp. 332–352; and Jerry Wexler and David Ritz, *Rhythm and the Blues: A Life in American Music* (1993), pp. 203–216, an overview written by Franklin's main producer, Wexler. Aretha Franklin and David Ritz, *From These Roots* (1999), is an autobiography.

PSYCHEDELIC ROCK

Tom Wolfe, *The Electric Kool-Aid Acid Test* (1968, reissued 2008), provides a firsthand account of the psychedelic culture that arose around Ken Kesey. Written in conjunction with the Rock and Roll Hall of Fame and Museum, James Henke and Parke Puterbaugh (eds.), *I Want to Take You Higher: The Psychedelic Era, 1965–1969* (1997), makes exhaustive use of photographs, posters, and other archival material. Jim DeRogatis, *Kaleidoscope Eyes: Psychedelic Rock from the '60s to the '90s* (1996), looks specifically at the music and traces its strands to the 1990s.

THE GRATEFUL DEAD

John Rocco and Brian Rocco (eds.), *Dead Reckonings: The Life and Times of the Grateful Dead* (1999), compiles the usual and offbeat tales, reviews, and interviews, including a bit from Miles Davis's autobiography. Rock Scully and David Dalton, *Living with the Dead: Twenty Years on the Bus with Garcia and the Grateful Dead* (1996), presents the memories and insights of the band's longtime road manager, Scully. David Gans, *Conversations with the Dead: The Grateful Dead Interview Book*, fully updated ed. (2002), gathers the most pertinent interview material. Robert Hunter, *A Box of Rain* (1990, reissued 1993), augments Hunter's collected lyrics with illustrations and memories. Jerry Garcia, *Harrington Street* (1995), collects guitarist leader Garcia's writings and art. Oliver Trager, *The American Book of the Dead: The Definitive Grateful Dead Encyclopedia* (1997), is the most comprehensive reference work on the Dead, with some 800 entries and many photos. David Shenk and Steve Silberman, *Skeleton Key: A Dictionary for Deadheads* (1994), is a smaller but useful compendium.

THE DOORS

Greil Marcus, *The Doors: A Lifetime of Listening to Five Mean Years*

(2011), is an extraordinary exploration of the legacy of the Doors by one of rock's preeminent critics and historians. Jim Morrison, *The Lords, and the New Creatures: Poems* (1970, reissued 1987), the first volume of Morrison's verse to be published, is earnest, frequently graphic, and by turns dark, sophomoric, and exuberant. Biographies of Morrison and the Doors include Jerry Hopkins and Daniel Sugerman, *No One Here Gets Out Alive* (1980, reissued 1997), one of the cornerstones of the Morrison myth-building empire but also the best and most revealing chronicle of the band's history; and James Riordan and Jerry Prochnicky, *Break on Through: The Life and Death of Jim Morrison* (1991).

JIMI HENDRIX

David Henderson, *'Scuse Me While I Kiss the Sky*, rev. ed. (1981, reissued 1996; originally published as *Jimi Hendrix: Voodoo Child of the Aquarian Age*, 1978), is a thoroughly researched though sometimes inelegant biography. Charles Shaar Murray, *Crosstown Traffic: Jimi Hendrix and Post-War Pop* (1989), presents a serious examination of Hendrix's life, work, and influence from musical, historical, and cultural perspectives. Tony Brown, *Jimi Hendrix: A Visual Documentary—His Life, Loves and Music* (1992), chronicles in detail the daily events of Hendrix's life and is copiously illustrated. Harry Shapiro and Caesar Glebbeek, *Jimi Hendrix: Electric Gypsy*, rev. and updated ed. (1995), is an informative biography augmented by a chronology, discography, and family tree. Charles R. Cross, *Room Full of Mirrors* (2005), offers a thorough account of Hendrix's life.

THE VELVET UNDERGROUND

M.C. Kostek, *The Velvet Underground Handbook* (1992), provides a detailed, annotated listing of the Velvet Underground's recordings, films, and related materials. Victor Bockris and Gerard Malanga, *Up-tight: The Velvet Underground Story*, new ed. (1995), is a definitive, talking-book account of the group's career from 1965 to 1970. Lou Reed, *Between Thought and Expression: Selected Lyrics of Lou Reed* (1991), includes several Velvet Underground songs.

Index